DATE DUE

W ECHNOLOGY
STARTER

GAYLORD   PRINTED IN U.S.A.

WEBMASTER
AND INFORMATION TECHNOLOGY

career starter

2nd edition

Joan Vaughn
with Jason R. Rich

New York

Library of Congress Cataloging-in-Publication Data:
Vaughn, Joan.
   Webmaster career starter / Joan Vaughn with Jason R. Rich—2nd ed.
     p. cm.
   ISBN 1-57685-371-3 (pbk.)
   1.Web site development—Vocational guidance. 2. Webmasters. I. Rich, Jason R.
   II. Title.
   TK5105.888.V38 2001
   005.2'76—dc21   2001029338

Printed in the United States of America
9 8 7 6 5 4 3 2 1
Second Edition

For more information or to place an order, contact LearningExpress at:
   900 Broadway
   Suite 604
   New York, NY 10003

Or visit us at:
   www.learnatest.com

Contents

Contents

Introduction

Why Enter the Information Technology Field?

THE INTERNET has become one of the fastest growing and most powerful communications tools in the world. Whether it's to send and receive e-mail, obtain information, shop online, participate in online chats, play multiplayer computer games, discover the latest news, or acquire new knowledge, the Internet and the World Wide Web have brought us all into the digital information age.

People from all walks of life can now connect to the Web from a personal computer, wireless PDA (personal digital assistant), cell phone, or through Web TV (that allows people to surf the Web via their television set). New technology is constantly being created to enhance connection speeds and how people surf the Web.

Meanwhile, a growing number of people are exploring cyberspace, whether it's for business or pleasure. As a result of this incredible explosion in the Internet's popularity, companies of all sizes and in all industries are scrambling not only to become established on the Web, but also to create a presence that will attract new customers, and make it easier to communicate with and service existing customers.

These days, it's not just dot-com companies (companies formed to do business on the Internet) or high-tech businesses that are in dire need of hiring talented people to create and manage websites—it's traditional businesses and organizations of all kinds.

Designing, creating, and managing a website typically requires a webmaster (someone to oversee the entire project) and often a team of talented people responsible for programming, creating graphics, developing content, and keeping the site operational. Many websites operated by businesses now incorporate much more than basic graphics and text. Because of this trend, companies need to hire employees to create and manage streaming video and audio, graphic animations, e-commerce applications (online shopping), and other forms of interactive content. These enhancements and applications then need to be brought together into an easy-to-use online environment. In addition, there are security matters, bandwidth (the rate at which data can be transferred) concerns, and countless other technical issues that people operating a website are responsible for overseeing.

Considering that thousands of existing businesses as well as many new online-based businesses are creating a presence on the Internet each and every week, a tremendous demand for skilled webmasters has emerged. If you have the right skills or choose to pursue the appropriate training, incredible job opportunities are available as a webmaster working for companies of all sizes, in all industries, and in cities across the United States and throughout the world.

So, whether you are looking for your first job or considering a career change, this book is for you! Every Internet-related article, research study, and salary survey indicates that the best jobs are currently in information technology. More specifically, within the information technology industry, the hottest jobs and the largest projected growth are in Web technology.

This book will show you how to become a part of the emerging Web technology field within a relatively short time (depending on the skills you already possess). You'll discover what types of jobs are available, how to obtain the training you need to land the best jobs, and find out exactly what it takes to become a webmaster or someone working in the information technologies field. After you become a qualified job applicant, this book will teach you how to find and ultimately land a job in this field. Most important, you'll learn how to develop a career path for yourself that will keep you up-to-date on emerging technologies in order to ensure you're always qualified to fill the best possible—and highest paying—job openings in your field.

Since this is still an emerging field, the requirements for entry aren't yet firmly established. While there are certainly specific skills a webmaster or someone working in the information technology (IT) field must have, people are moving into these careers from many other occupations and professions. Graphic artists, writers, animators, programmers, producers, marketers, people in the financial field, and even musicians all possess skills that can be extremely useful to a webmaster. As you'll soon learn, people who bring such skills to jobs in this field will certainly find themselves at an advantage and in demand by employers.

Being a good webmaster requires more than just being able to plan, create, program, and maintain a website. If you're operating a site, having a thorough understanding of that business and the industry it's in as well as effective communication with employees, customers, clients, and others using the Web are also necessary.

To get the most out of this book, take a moment to look at what you will find in each chapter:

Chapter	Description
One **The Hottest Jobs and** **How to Get Them**	This chapter will help you decide if a webmaster career is a good choice for you. It defines the term *webmaster,* describes other related IT jobs, and provides an overview of typical job responsibilities. It also contains salary surveys and other industry statistics.
Two **All about Training Programs**	This chapter will help you decide which type of training program is most appropriate for your needs and plans. It describes a variety of training programs and provides sample course descriptions.
Three **Directory of Training** **Programs and Financial Aid:** **Discovering the Possibilities**	Once you have decided what type of training you want, this chapter will provide you with more information about schools that offer computer-related academic programs and vendor-training programs. This chapter also provides you with all the information you need to know about securing financial aid for the training program of your choice.

WEBMASTER AND INFORMATION TECHNOLOGY CAREER STARTER

CHAPTER one

THE HOTTEST JOBS AND HOW TO GET THEM

THIS CHAPTER defines the term *webmaster* and outlines the various tasks people with this job title are expected to perform. It also gives you an overview of the web development market and the range of salaries available in the field. Finally, this chapter provides a self-evaluation quiz to help you decide if becoming a webmaster—or someone working in the information technologies field—is a good career choice for you.

THE INTERNET has become the most effective and fastest-growing means of advertising, shopping, research, and communication in the world today. Since the Web is such a vital part of business, the people who develop and maintain the Web have become critical workers in the worldwide job market. But who are these people? What do they really do?

The most common job title for someone who develops and maintains information on the Internet is webmaster. This is typically the person who is in charge of a company's website or online presence. This might mean doing hands-on work to develop or maintain a site, or overseeing a team of professionals with specific areas of expertise, such as programming, graphic design, animation, content development (writers/editors), illustrators, musicians, videographers, and so on.

Like all new terms, webmaster is quickly becoming overused and misunderstood—in part, because this is an emerging field and the actual role and job responsibilities of a webmaster vary greatly from company to company.

Technically speaking, anyone who has a personal Web page is a webmaster. In the business world, however, this title is given to the person who is actually in charge of all aspects of a website's operation. Working under the webmaster are often many people with a diverse set of specialized skills. These jobs are often considered to be within the information technologies (IT) field, although some require specialized skills from related fields, such as graphic design, advertising, or marketing. The information technologies field focuses on disseminating any type of information or data using technology and the Internet.

ROLES AND RESPONSIBILITIES

In a business environment, typically more than one person is responsible for designing, developing, and maintaining a website. This table will give you an idea of the people who are often in charge of getting a company's website up and running:

Role	Description of Activities
Information Architect	■ Gathers and analyzes requirements for a website ■ Designs the navigation scheme for a website ■ Analyzes requests for website enhancements to determine placement ■ Creates and maintains business processes for a website
Graphic Designer/ Interface Engineer	■ Creates the initial look and feel for the website ■ Works with content/page developers on the individual design of pages ■ Develops the user interface that surfers use to navigate the website as well as the overall look and feel of the site

Content/Page Developer	▧ Creates the pages that reside on a website, including all text, graphics, and other aspects.
	▧ Keeps the content current
Web Technologist/	▧ Configures and manages the Web server
Support Analyst/	▧ Selects end-user tools such as browser and
Network Administrators/	Web editor compatibility
Network Engineers	▧ Writes scripts and programs to be used through the browser
	▧ Provides and monitors Web usage statistics (traffic)
	▧ Maintains the site's technical operation
Producer/Creative Director	▧ Responsible for creating or overseeing the production of a website, including animation, video or audio elements, and design
	▧ Works closely with editorial (content), marketing, and technology staff to create user-friendly, efficient Web pages
E-Commerce Director	▧ Responsible for creating and maintaining the e-commerce or online shopping aspect of a website
Wireless Software Engineer	▧ Responsible for developing ways for people using wireless devices, such as PDAs or cellular phones, to utilize a website

A DESCRIPTION OF EACH ROLE

Each role is vital and requires a unique set of skills; it is important to note that job titles and job roles vary greatly from company to company. The examples we give here should serve as an indication of what each job *might* entail. However, it is impossible to pin down an exact job description that will fit with every company since IT professionals with similar titles sometimes perform different roles depending upon the company for whom they work.

An information architect, for example, ensures that the site is easy to use, that the customers can find what they want, and that it's meeting the needs of the intended audience. An information architect needs to be an expert in customer requirements, communication, and rhetorical analysis.

A graphic designer or interface engineer also plays a significant role because he or she must make the site aesthetically appealing to the intended audience, while ensuring its rapid performance speed. A graphic artist dedicated to Web development must possess all of the expertise of a regular graphic artist—audience analysis, color and shape theory, creativity—and also understand the technology and theory unique to creating graphics for the Web.

The content and page developers are the subject matter experts. These people are responsible for creating the ideas, choosing how they are to be conveyed, and then for translating—or overseeing the translation of—the content into actual Web pages using HTML, Java, C++, Flash, and other programming and Web design tools and languages. It is very important to have knowledgeable people working as content developers since the information on a website is usually about a particular aspect of a business. The content developers must have expertise in the services and products of the business that owns the site as well as Web technology. This type of job typically requires strong written communication skills, since content developers work as writers, editors, marketers, advertisers, and artists in order to ensure that the message a website conveys actually does its job.

A Web technologist is crucial to the success of a website. Lacking a technologist to code scripts and create interactive, online-based applications, a website would only function as a place to post unchanging text, which does not provide a competitive advantage for the company. A Web technologist must be an expert in general Web technology, Web servers, and coding in Web languages.

Producers and creative directors are usually in charge of not only producing all the front end of a website, but also utilizing the latest website development tools to incorporate streaming video, audio, animation, and other technologies into a site—not just to make it more visually pleasing to the visitor, but to make it a more powerful tool for communicating information, selling, marketing, or educating.

Since e-commerce is becoming a booming business, e-commerce directors are in demand. More and more people are shopping on the Internet, and a growing number of companies are looking to expand their market share and reach by catering to Web surfers across the country and the world. E-commerce directors add applications to a website to make it possible for visitors to shop online, place orders, obtain customer service, and communicate with a company without ever picking up a telephone or visiting a retail store.

Support Analysts, sometimes called Network Administrators, work with a company's servers. Servers must be constantly maintained and updated and users need consistent and reliable access websites, so someone who is responsible for maintaining the servers must make sure all network communication is functioning properly. They might also check scripts, assign user rights, and implement security policies, in addition to other varied responsibilities.

Network engineers must configure the network. They are responsible for designing and implementing the network. Their focus is the physical side of the network; they design how the network enables communication between computers. The cornerstone of a good network engineer is that he or she be able to adjust to the ever-changing needs of the users.

There are also security concerns involved with operating and maintaining a website, especially when classified data—such as credit card information from customers—passwords, or financial data are involved. Internet security has become an occupation unto itself, especially with the threat of hackers, computer viruses, and online credit card fraud that exists in cyberspace.

WHO FULFILLS THESE ROLES?

Depending on the company, the industry, and the underlying purpose of a company's website, in some instances, one or two people perform all of the Web design and maintenance roles. In other situations—especially for online-based companies, dot-com businesses, and larger traditional companies with a strong Web presence—a Web/information technologies department is staffed by many specialists—writers, programmers, animators, designers, producers, editors, and so on.

In most large companies, the technology department has a manager, a technology expert, a graphic designer, an information architect, and at least a few content developers. On the other hand, in a small company, sometimes the entire department consists of just one person.

The Webmaster's Guild found on the Association of Internet Professionals website (www.webmaster.org) defines webmaster in this way: "The goal of a webmaster is to design, implement, and maintain an effective site on the

World Wide Web. To achieve this, a webmaster must possess knowledge of fields as diverse as network configuration, interface and graphic design, software development, business strategy, writing, marketing, and project management. Because the function of a webmaster encompasses so many areas, the position is sometimes held by a team of individuals."

An Internet dictionary (www.pcwebopaedia.com/webmaster.htm) defines webmaster in this way: "An individual who manages a website." Given that definition, a webmaster might be responsible for:

- ▶ ensuring Web server hardware and software runs correctly
- ▶ designing a website
- ▶ both creating and updating Web pages for the website
- ▶ handling feedback from site visitors
- ▶ creating Common Gateway Interface (CGI) scripts
- ▶ monitoring site traffic

A Web Week study lists the following as the most common tasks a webmaster performs:

- ▶ answers visitor questions
- ▶ compiles and analyzes hit statistics
- ▶ maintains Web pages
- ▶ plans how a website fits into overall company strategy
- ▶ designs Web pages

THE WEBMASTER

In companies where one person manages every aspect of a website, that person is called the webmaster. In larger Web groups, the person previously described as the technologist—the one who designs and manages servers, writes scripts and applications—is generally called the webmaster.

In this book, we will concentrate on the education and training needed for the technological aspects of Web design. We will not discuss the training needed for the roles of information architect, graphic designer, or content developer. To fill many of these positions, industry-specific skills and knowledge outside of the computer field are required. For example, working as a content developer may require a journalism degree.

WHERE DO WEBMASTERS WORK?

There are three main types of places for a Webmaster to work:

1. *Companies that create and manage websites as a business.* Many companies don't have the staff or the space to create and maintain websites themselves, so they hire companies, like WinMill, Razorfish, or New York Interactive, that have the staff, technological know-how, and expertise to build, design, and maintain websites.

2. *Traditional companies that have developed an Internet presence in order to expand its market or better serve customers.* These companies can be in any industry and conduct any type of business. Any business you can think of probably has a website that's operated by a webmaster and a team of information technology professionals. AT&T, The Gap, JiffyLube, H&R Block, Fidelity Investments, and The Walt Disney Company are just a small sampling of traditional companies with a presence on the Web.

3. *Online-based businesses (dot-com companies and high-tech firms) that operate exclusively on the World Wide Web.* Amazon.com, Excite.com, and Yahoo.com are examples of popular dot-com companies that exist only on the Web. Some online-based companies may be consumer-driven like Amazon; however, companies such as Yahoo! and Excite maintain business through advertising and investors rather than actually operate via e-commerce.

COMPANIES THAT CREATE AND MANAGE WEBSITES AS A BUSINESS

There are two types of companies that focus on websites: an independent website development company and an Internet Service Provider (ISP). A website development company creates sites for other companies. These firms have teams of people on hand to meet the site development needs of virtually any business.

In a Web development company, a webmaster's main activities involve assessing a customer's current network, suggesting technology, designing interactive pages, and writing applications that users access online using a Web browser. Companies that don't want to, don't have the space to, or can't afford to hire the staff necessary to design and maintain a website in-house typically outsource these responsibilities to a website development company.

Sometimes, an ISP manages websites for other companies. In this case, the ISP owns the servers and hardware that the website uses. The duties of a webmaster at an ISP would include:

- ▶ ensuring that the website is set up correctly
- ▶ confirming that the servers and connection lines work properly
- ▶ providing statistics about the website's use to customers

Since the Internet has become such an important tool for medium-to-large-sized businesses, many companies are bringing their website development efforts in-house in order to maintain maximum control and eliminate reliance on outside companies. This desire for control has greatly increased the demand for qualified webmasters and information technology professionals.

COMPANIES THAT USE WEBSITES TO DO THEIR BUSINESS

A webmaster might also work for a traditional or online-based (dot-com) company that utilizes Web technology to do business. This includes product and service companies, schools, hospitals, and just about any other type of business you can think of, in virtually every industry. These businesses might use Web technology in three different ways: Internet, intranet, and extranet.

1. An Internet site is one available on the World Wide Web. Businesses use Internet websites, for example, to advertise their products and services, to distribute information, or for e-commerce applications.
2. An Intranet site is one available only to employees of a company on a network. An intranet is a very effective method for communicating with a large number of employees. Companies use intranet sites to do

everything from publishing corporate news, to posting procedures, to letting employees change their benefits options.

3. An extranet is a secured connection where special customers can use the Internet to enter a special, secured area where they can do business. An extranet is often used for placing orders and electronic data interchange (EDI).

   Companies need webmasters to design and manage the technology for all three types of sites.

HOT INTERNET SITES FOR WEBMASTERS

Here are some websites dedicated to the art and science of being a webmaster. To learn more about this field, determine what types of jobs are available, what skills or knowledge you'll need to acquire to enter this field, and what types of industries you might be suited to work in, visit some or all of these sites. Also, refer to Appendix A for a listing of professional organizations and Appendix B for additional resources available to the would-be webmaster.

World Wide Web Consortium	www.w3.org
CIO WebBusiness	http://webbusiness.cio.com
The Web Career Research Center	www.cio.com/forums/careers
Webmasters Seminars Inc.	www.Webmasterseminars.com
HotWired's Webmonkey	www.hotwired.com/webmonkey
Netologist	www.netologist.net
SitePort	www.sitepoint.com
Webmaster Central	www.wmcentral.com
The Webmaster's Net	www.thewebmasters.net

SAMPLE JOB DESCRIPTIONS

The following job descriptions were modeled on submissions from a variety of Internet-based career-oriented websites—such as The Monster Board, www.monster.com. From these sample job descriptions and help wanted ads, you'll learn more about what employers are looking for.

Job Description #1
Site Master

We are looking for site managers who will assume day-to-day ownership of sites similar to ABC Tech's. Our site managers are responsible for approximately two sites. The ideal candidate will work closely with editorial, marketing, and technology to manage multiple projects.

Site managers must be creative, entrepreneurial, flexible, and team-oriented. Knowledge of streaming media, online music, wireless, and Net markets is also helpful.

Responsibilities:

- Make editorial decisions about site content
- Day-to-day maintenance and functionality of sites
- Edit, research, and plot data charts and tables
- Write press releases
- Create PowerPoint presentations
- Make transcripts of conferences
- Write headlines
- Create some original content
- Light copy or line editing
- Gather news and press releases

The ideal candidate will implement site functionality, monitor message boards and site traffic, and so on. Driving traffic to the site and other aspects of the business are also tasks the candidate must have experience completing. The site manager must ensure that the content and user experience on the site is high quality.

Requirements:

Candidate must be familiar with Web publishing and Web development. Advanced domain expertise will also be taken into account. Site managers also should have some knowledge of:

- HTML coding
- Website graphic design using Adobe Photoshop
- Converting files into PDF
- MS Office

Job Description #2
Webmaster/Producer

As one of New York City's leading weekly entertainment publishers, *Be Entertained* gives the city's residents more than 2,000 ideas on how to spend their free time. First published in 1995, *Be Entertained* provides features, news, reviews, previews, interviews, and hundreds of in-depth listings that are informative and entertaining to read.

Be Entertained is currently looking for a talented Webmaster/Producer to join our online team, which is responsible for the maintenance of the *Be Entertained* website. This is a great opportunity for a motivated, problem-solving individual to contribute to the company.

The job will entail maintaining site content in a variety of formats. Updating and maintaining the *Be Entertained* website's functionality, tracking and reporting website usage, serving ads, researching tools and services, and monitoring security are also part of the job. The Webmaster/Producer must also monitor production flow among the advertising, editorial, and design elements of the site and review content prior to publishing to ensure the quality of the data posted to the site.

The ideal candidate must also review and recommend appropriate modifications to the site and be responsible for the website's daily operation, efficiency, and functionality. He/she will also be the primary technical resource for the online group, planning and administering the website's technical infrastructure.

Excellent project management and communication skills are necessary. Candidate must be detail-oriented and possess strong organizational skills, excellent written and verbal skills, and the ability to communicate effectively.

Skills required for this position include:

- Linux
- Apache
- Mac OS
- Adobe Photoshop
- Adobe GoLive

Candidate must be familiar with:

- Quark Xpress
- FileMaker
- MySQL
- Web Server Administration
- JavaScript

Job Description #3
Webmaster

ABC Talent Agency) has an opening for an experienced webmaster who will be responsible for developing, maintaining, deploying, and troubleshooting the agency's production
and development Apache server installation. Additional responsibilities include deploying
NetLedger code into production and supporting the development/QA organizations during
the release cycle. Webmaster must be on call during off hours and cope with a fast-paced
environment.

Duties:

- Installing, configuring, and administering Apache Web servers in a production
  environment
- Working with Jserv
- Implementing SSL (secure socket layers) with Apache (mod_ssl, OpenSSL)
- Working on some variety of Unix
- Programming experience, Java/C++ a must

Skills:

- Familiarity with Linux
- Oracle
- QA/process background
- Fast learner
- Good written and verbal communicator

Job Description #4
Webmaster/eBusiness Project Manager

Ideal candidate will define, develop, and manage the system roadmap for externally facing web initiatives. Webmaster will also manage teams of 2–6 Java developers and work
jointly with the IS&T organization to ensure business requirements are clearly commu-
nicated. In addition, webmaster will manage all usability testing sessions for each new
release.

Required:

- MBA and 4-6 years combined IT and system implementation experience
- Strong project management, communication, and presentation skills
- Experience in defining and managing system roadmaps for new functionality and integration into existing systems
- Experience with business process analysis and design
- Experience leading teams and ability to complete projects in a particular timeframe

Desired Skills:

Candidate should have background in IT project management and system implementation. He or she must also be creative and possess problem-solving skills.

Candidate must have Web development experience with Java, ATG Dynamo, CORBA, HTML, CGI, Perl. Experience with Messaging and Middleware architecture is a must. Experience with general business applications and a good understanding of their Web, high availability, and computing requirements are required. Candidate must be able to prioritize multiple requirements from various organizations, and communicate to senior management the status and future direction of the system.

Job Description #5
Webmaster

If you are a seasoned webmaster with a complete and clear understanding of Internet, intranet, and extranet design and development, please contact me immediately.

Candidate must be familiar with the following technologies: Broadvision, HTML, ASP, JavaScript (client side),VB Script (server side), Microsoft Visual InterDev, Microsoft Visual SourceSafe, Microsoft FrontPage, Microsoft SQL, Access, Database integration, Microsoft IIS.

Responsibilities:

- Recommend and implement site improvements
- Act as primary point of contact for company
- Provide assistance to the design team

- Research, assess, and recommend new technologies
- Develop and implement deployment procedures
- Track and report site traffic

Candidate must be familiar with staging and production environment procedures.

WHY BECOME A WEBMASTER? THE FUTURE OUTLOOK

The computer industry has grown rapidly over the past two decades and this growth has created a need for highly skilled computer experts. The U.S. Department of Labor's 2000–2001 statistics list computer services as the fastest growing industry in the next decade. They report, "As computer applications continue to expand, these occupations are projected to be the fastest growing and rank among the top 20 in the number of new jobs created over the 1998–2008 period."

The demand for webmasters will rise even faster than other computer-related jobs because of the recent widespread use and development of the Internet. As Web technology becomes more sophisticated, webmasters will need to upgrade their skills, technical expertise, and ability to interact with users. Webmasters need to remain flexible in order to stay competitive in the job market. Experts suggest that the successful employees of the future will be those dedicated to continuous improvement just to keep up with the changes in the industry's future.

SALARIES: WHAT WEBMASTERS EARN

There are a number of factors that affect salaries in any industry. Among them are supply and demand, employer size, corporate industry, and geographic location.

The Department of Labor provides specific information about computer programmers and system analysts; webmaster tasks certainly fall into both categories.

	Computer Programmers	System Analysts
Median earnings 1999	$47,550	$46,670
Lowest 10%	Less than $27,670	Less than $26,690
Highest 10%	More than $88,730	More than $87,730

For more detailed salary information for a particular job title in a particular city or geographic region, Salary.com (www.salary.com) is an excellent resource.

For a webmaster working in New York City in early 2001, Salary.com reports, "A typical webmaster working in metro New York, New York is expected to earn a median base salary of $61,390. Half of the people in this job are expected to earn between $53,231 and $75,922 (i.e., between the 25th and 75th percentiles). These numbers are based on national averages adjusted by geographic salary differentials."

For a similar job in San Francisco, for example, Salary.com reports, "A typical webmaster working in metro California (San Francisco) is expected to earn a median base salary of $62,028. Half of the people in this job are expected to earn between $53,784 and $76,711 (i.e., between the 25th and 75th percentiles). These numbers are based on national averages adjusted by geographic salary differentials."

Meanwhile, a webmaster's position in Houston, Texas offers the following salary range, according to Salary.com, "A typical webmaster working in metro Texas (Houston) is expected to earn a median base salary of $55,277. Half of the people in this job are expected to earn between $47,931 and $68,363 (i.e., between the 25th and 75th percentiles). These numbers are based on national averages adjusted by geographic salary differentials."

IS A WEBMASTER CAREER RIGHT FOR YOU?

Now that you have some understanding of all the different things a webmaster might do, what the job market demands, and the salary potential, let's take a look at whether you should join this exciting field. The following self-assessment quiz will help you determine if this is the right field for you.

Do You Have What It Takes to Be a Webmaster?

Webmasters must be able to think logically, understand networking and Web technology, and interpret a customer's needs. They must also have a thorough understanding of the company and the industry in which they're working; plus, a webmaster should stay informed on the latest technological advancements and developments. In addition, they must be extremely creative, somewhat artistic, and have excellent written communication skills.

The following are some basic questions designed for someone who currently possesses just a little bit of computer knowledge, but who might be interested in pursuing the training required to enter into both the IT and webmaster fields. For someone who has some technical knowledge, you'll want to ask yourself more detailed questions, such as what specific skills you need to acquire and what type of company you'd like to work for. These issues, however, will be addressed in later chapters.

	Yes	No
Do you own or have access to a personal computer?	___	___
Do you enjoy trying out new software packages?	___	___
Do you use the Internet to find information, educate yourself, or for entertainment purposes?	___	___
Have you ever placed an order or done any other type of business over the Internet?	___	___
Have you ever removed the cover from your computer just to see what was inside?	___	___
Have you ever been frustrated by your computer's lack of processing speed and then done something about it?	___	___
Do you enjoy talking to people—even people who disagree with you?	___	___
Do you spend your free time solving problems and puzzles?	___	___
Do you have strong written and verbal communication skills?	___	___
Do you have what it takes to combine text, graphics, sound, and other interactive elements to communicate information in a clear way?	___	___
When faced with a subject that you don't understand, do you keep at it until you learn it?	___	___
Do you cope well with change, reacting favorably to it instead of becoming frustrated by it?	___	___

Do you love to learn? Do you have the motivation to learn
new skills and obtain new knowledge on your own? ____ ____

Do others consider you to be a "tinkerer"? Are you often able to
devise non-traditional solutions to problems you face at work? ____ ____

Are you fascinated by the new and ever-changing ways people are
able to communicate using the World Wide Web? Does the use
of this technology inspire you? ____ ____

Do you currently read any computer industry news? ____ ____

If you answered "yes" to several of these questions, chances are you will feel right at home in an industry as challenging and diverse as the World Wide Web.

THE INSIDE TRACK

Who: John DePalm

What: Vice President, Database and Customer Information

Where: Primedia Magazine and Internet Group

INSIDER'S STORY

When I was going to high school in Puerto Rico, I was interested in aerospace engineering. My first college course in that curriculum was a computer class, and right away I said, "This is neat." I've been hooked ever since.

My first job was as a programmer/analyst at Tri-Star Pictures, and it was 50-50 between mainframes and PCs. I didn't like working with mainframes—it was too rigid for me. So I decided to focus on desktops, because that's where I saw the future going.

In my current position, I'm asked to draw on both my managerial and technological expertise to achieve quantifiable measures of success. I need to be acutely aware of our business and financial requirements, translate them into technological project plans, and pass them along to the programmers.

Technology is always providing new challenges. There's something to be learned every day. That's a cliché, but it's very true. You need to stay on top of changes all the time. It moves so fast, and that's the thing that excites me about it.

My path has been to do a little bit of everything—some programming, some corporate training, some sales support, and some infrastructure building. I'd recommend that strategy to anyone—don't get stuck in a small niche. Technology moves very quickly, and in the long run it's better to keep your skill set diversified.

INSIDER'S ADVICE

As in any profession, you won't know everything. With that in mind, it's best to try to build and become part of a team of experts. At your core, have an expertise in a couple of things, and collaborate with that team. Sometimes you need to put your pride on the shelf and ask someone a question. When you need to, draw on the knowledge of others instead of banging your head against a wall. Don't feel that you're alone.

CHAPTER two

ALL ABOUT TRAINING PROGRAMS

BEFORE YOU can begin your career as a webmaster or an IT professional, you'll need to acquire the necessary training. You'll need to learn how to use the latest technology to create and manage cutting-edge websites. In this chapter, you'll discover how and where to obtain the necessary training, how to choose the training program that's right for you, and how to get the most out of the program you choose to pursue.

AS YOU'LL SOON discover, cyberspace is an exciting place to visit. Millions upon millions of people make their way through this high-tech virtual world each and every day. Those who keep the Internet running are the many webmasters who utilize the latest technology and programming techniques to create interactive online experiences for Web surfers. With more and more companies establishing a presence on the Web, the need for highly qualified webmasters is expanding by the day.

In order to land the best possible job, you'll need to obtain the necessary training so that you're fully qualified to meet the ever-expanding needs of corporate America when it comes to establishing, designing, and maintaining a presence on the Web. Simply understanding how to use a Web page design and publishing program such as Microsoft FrontPage 2000 is not enough.

Once you decide to pursue a career as a webmaster, you'll need to choose what type of training will help you acquire the knowledge you need to succeed. There are many types of training programs available. Some are classroom based, while others utilize online learning (interactive multimedia), videos, or other forms of self-paced distance learning (textbooks, cassettes, and so on.). Obtaining training will require a commitment of your time and money. Some of the things you'll want to consider as you evaluate your options include:

▶ how to choose the right kind of training
▶ how to choose the right length of training
▶ what to do to make your training experience the most successful it can be

PLANNING: BEFORE YOU BEGIN YOUR TRAINING PROGRAM

The following steps will help you create the best possible game plan for yourself as you select the best training program(s) to participate in. Consider what type of training you need and what your ultimate career goals are. Focus on pursuing the training that will lead you toward achieving your goals. For more guidance on creating and attaining career goals, take a look at *Your Career: Coach Yourself to Success* (Jason R. Rich, LearningExpress, 2001). By determining your personal, professional, and financial goals first, you'll then be able to figure out exactly what training you need and find the best ways of obtaining that knowledge and skill set.

1. Make sure that you have a high school diploma or a GED.

A career as a webmaster does not always require a college education; however, a high school diploma or a GED is almost always required. Landing a job at a major corporation within the Management Information Systems (MIS) or information technologies department will typically require a college degree and possibly even an advanced degree or professional certification.

▶ If you're in high school now, there are a number of ways you can prepare for your professional future. A career in computers requires good analytical and problem-solving skills. Taking computer, math, and science classes will help you attain these skills. Learn as much about computers as you can both in school and on your own. Focus on learning about off-the-shelf computer programs as well as about operating systems and programming languages. If your interests truly lie in IT and career opportunities that relate to the Internet and the World Wide Web, spend time learning how to design websites using popular programming tools and languages, such as FrontPage 2000, Flash, Java, C++, and HTML.

▶ If you want to change careers, take an inventory of your computer skills. Do you already have the skills you will need for this new career or will you need additional training? In your current job, do you have access to a computer? Are you the one that your coworkers come to for help when they have problems with their hardware or software? Does your company link its computers together via a LAN (local area network)? If so, do you understand the technologies used to achieve this link? Do you use the Internet frequently? Have you developed your own personal website? Many people who are changing from one computer-related field to another will answer these questions positively.

▶ Consider pursing a college education and majoring in computers and/or information technology. Obtaining an advanced degree will make you a more valuable asset to a future employer and greatly increase your earning potential.

▶ While you're still in school (high school or college), participate in an internship program and obtain as much hands-on real-world experience as you can.

In New York City, a group called the New York New Media Association offers an internship program for those looking to gain experience, and perhaps entry into "new media" (the information technology industry). For more information—or to read about available internships—check out their website: www.nynma-internship.org. For information about internships in other cities, try a search on any search engine (Google.com, Dogpile.com, and so on) for internship job boards, or check out job hunting websites, such as HotJobs or the Monster Board. Use the search word "internship."

2. Learn about the computer industry.

If you are interested in a career as a webmaster, you can begin preparing right now by following these simple guidelines.

▶ Take advantage of any opportunity to work with a computer—at home, work, school, or at the library. Also, learn as much as you can about the Internet and how websites work. As you become familiar with how to create a basic website, explore topics, such as animation (Flash), streaming media (audio and video), electronic publishing, e-commerce, and online security.

▶ Read about computers and computer professionals in newspapers, books, and magazines. Study the latest trends. Learn about new developments. Read critically and ask questions about each article. You may not be able to answer those questions now, but you will later. Reading industry-oriented publications, such as *InfoWorld* and *The Industry Standard*, will help keep you informed about the latest developments in Internet-related technologies.

▶ Join a computer club at school or in your community. It is a great way to keep up-to-date on the latest developments.

▶ Talk to people employed in the field. Do you know someone who works with computers? Perhaps he or she will sit down with you and tell you about the field. Find out the advantages and disadvantages associated with the person's job.

▶ Participate in an internship program and work for a company with a strong online presence. Try to spend time working directly with the people responsible for designing, creating, and maintaining a company's website or online presence.

WHY SHOULD YOU GET TRAINING?

If you want to land the best possible job and have job security in this fast-changing industry, you'll need to have the skills that are in demand by employers. Once you obtain the core knowledge you need to get started, you'll be able to supplement that training by participating in ongoing classes, reading manuals, attending trade shows, watching instructional videotapes, participating in professional associations, or taking online-based distance learning classes. The fact is, to be successful in this field, once your training begins, it should never end—especially because programs can quickly become obsolete. Companies' needs are ever-changing; thus Microsoft, Apple, and other companies (Oracle, Novell, Allaire, and so on) are constantly creating new standards for the way the world communicates over the Internet. Although the structure of the Internet is basically consistent and reliable, new pieces of the puzzle are always added to the equation.

THE COMPETITIVE JOB MARKET

As with emerging jobs in any new field, in recent years it was very easy to get into IT without training while the industry was still being defined. Right now it is fairly easy to get an entry-level job in the IT field with only minimal training, but this is changing rapidly. More and more companies are relying on the Internet to conduct their businesses, which means they're requiring highly trained and knowledgeable people to manage their computer systems. Breaking into this industry now will require you to be able to demonstrate a proficiency using industry-standard tools and technologies.

As the World Wide Web gets more established, a wide range of training programs have been developed to address industry needs. With many training programs in place, the webmaster without formal training is at a major disadvantage.

First, you'll be competing against many job applicants who have advanced degrees in computer science or information technology. Second, now that formal training has become the norm, companies have started to mandate that webmasters have a degree or professional certificate.

Your formal training—whether you pursue a two- or four-year degree or a professional certificate (that you can often complete in a few months)— plus your experience will keep you competitive in your field for the years to come.

HOW TO EVALUATE TRAINING PROGRAMS

Schools are businesses; they need students in order to make money. When you think of it in that light, the brochure you read about a school is actually an advertisement. You, as a consumer, need to carefully research, evaluate, and compare schools the same way you would if you were buying a car or major appliance.

Come up with a list of criteria for judging a school or training program's worth to you. For instance, do you want to attend classes full time or part time? Are you more comfortable in a rural or urban setting? What kind of student–teacher ratio are you looking for? All of this information is available through a number of sources, including the schools themselves. Make a chart like the one below to help you compare the choices and make your decision.

According to an article entitled "Training for Transitions," by Lynn Breymer (published on Techies.com), "You don't need to be a programming guru to be a tech professional. There is a wide variety of careers revolving around technology that doesn't involve writing code, doing server maintenance, or creating database tables. Other tech-specific but non-programming career paths include human resources for tech employees, technical writing, and graphic design. . . . You can deduct as much as $1,500 for out-of-pocket postsecondary education costs with the new Hope tax credit. In addition, the federal government offers a lifetime-learning tax credit, which entails deductions as high as $1,000."

My Criteria	School A	School B	School C	School D
Rural setting	X	X		
Public school	X	X	X	X
Computer lab open 24 hours	X			X
Computer lab has PC and UNIX platforms	X		X	
Computer lab hires students	X			X
Student body size less than 10,000		X		X
Student-to-teacher ratio less than 10 to 1		X		X
Coed campus	X	X	X	X
Financial aid offered through the school			X	
Work-study program available	X	X	X	X
On-campus placement office	X	X		X
Large non-traditional student population			X	

If you have time, visit the schools in your area and talk to the guidance counselors. These counselors are trained to help you identify your needs and decide if their schools will meet your criteria. Follow this checklist in preparing for an on-campus visit:

▶ Contact the Office of Admissions at each school and make an appointment to visit. Be sure to request a complete tour as well as a meeting with a representative from the school who will be able to answer your questions. Remember to ask for the name of the person making the appointment and the person you will be meeting with.

▶ Bring a copy of your transcript or permanent record card if you will have the opportunity to meet with an admission counselor during your visit.

▶ Include a list of honors or awards you have received in school or the community.

▶ Know your PSAT and ACT or SAT test scores in case someone asks you about them.

▶ Be ready to ask questions about the school and surrounding community, especially about extracurricular activities and work opportunities, as well as other details you won't find in promotional brochures.

QUESTIONS TO ASK ABOUT TRAINING PROGRAMS

Is the Program Accredited?

The accreditation process recognizes schools and professional programs that provide a level of performance, integrity, and quality to its students and the community. The accreditation process is voluntary and is granted on the basis of the school's curriculum, staff ratios, and other criteria established by the accrediting agencies. Accreditation doesn't attempt to rank or grade the schools, only to accredit them.

So what does that mean to you? Basically, it assures you—and your potential employers—that the school you chose to attend tries to provide valuable courses taught by qualified instructors. In short, it offers you peace of mind.

Three national accreditation agencies and six regional agencies have jurisdiction over the entire United States; schools can also be accredited by professional organizations. Though a school can be accredited by more than one agency, one is enough. Most schools are proud of their accredited status and freely share the information in their printed materials, but you can be sure of their status by asking.

In addition to being state or nationally accredited, a school may be accredited by a company such as Microsoft, to train students in the use of their various products. For example, across the United States, Microsoft offers Microsoft Certified Technical Education Centers that are full-service training facilities offering state-of-the-art classrooms and highly trained instructors.

At these training centers, students can earn the following certificates:

▶ Microsoft Certified Professional
▶ Microsoft Certified Solution Developer
▶ Microsoft Certified Systems Engineer
▶ Microsoft Certified Systems Engineer with a specialty in the Internet
▶ Microsoft Certified Database Administrator
▶ Microsoft Certified Trainer

As someone interested in pursuing a career in webmaster and information technology, the Microsoft Certified Systems Engineer with a specialty in the Internet program may be an excellent educational path for you to obtain the initial training you'll need. Additional information about these programs is offered later; however, you can also call 800-636-7544 or e-mail mcp@msprograms.com for more information directly from Microsoft.

What Is the Program's Length?

You have several choices about the amount of time you spend on your training. Decide in advance how long you want to spend on your training and find a program that meets your needs and budget. Keep in mind, in addition to structured, classroom-based training programs, you can also participate in distance learning programs that are self-paced and allow you to work around your existing schedule.

These distance learning programs are available using textbooks, videotaped courses, audiotaped courses, and online (multimedia) courses. The curriculum is typically identical to what you'd learn in a traditional classroom environment; however, the approach to teaching is different. In terms of tuition, distance learning programs also tend to be cheaper.

What Is the Student–Teacher Ratio?

The student–teacher ratio is a statistic that shows the average number of students assigned to one teacher in a classroom or lab. It is important to know the ratio because a lower student-teacher ratio means that, as a student, you will get more small-group, one-on-one, intense training.

A higher ratio (30 to 1 or even 100 to 1) is sometimes acceptable for a lecture class in which interaction between students and teachers is not necessary. However, for a lab setting (hands-on work), students need a lower student–teacher ratio: 30 to 1 might be acceptable for easy work, 15 to 1 for moderate projects; intense work might require a 5 to 1 or even 1 to 1 ratio.

What Is the Classroom–Lab Ratio?

Theory and discussion, which you will get in a classroom setting, are important. However, lab experience—working hands-on with hardware and software—is equally important in a technical degree program. Evaluate how much of your training time will be spent in the classroom versus the lab. Be cautious about any program that does not include significant lab work. Lab work is an absolute must for acquiring hands-on experience as opposed to theoretical knowledge.

Is the School's Lab Technologically Advanced?

Technology is changing rapidly; it would be a waste to have excellent student–teacher ratios in a lab full of old technology. While it is important to become familiar with hardware and software that is a few years old—your future employer probably has some old equipment—you need to be sure that you will also have experience working with state-of-the-art equipment.

Investigate how the labs in your prospective schools are equipped, maintained, and updated. Through research, you can determine exactly what software and equipment the employers you'd like to work for are currently using, and then ensure that you will be taught using that equipment. You want to make sure you're not only being taught on the latest computer hardware, but you're also being trained to use the latest versions of the most popular operating systems, Web development tools, software packages, and Web programming languages (Java, HTML, C++, Flash, and so on.).

What Are the School's Job-Placement Statistics?

Most schools and programs have specific placement offices, dedicated to helping you find a job after you have completed your training. Placement offices keep records of what types of jobs their students get. Don't just read the statistics; closely examine them.

Understand the difference between a statistic that shows how many students got jobs in the computer field and one that shows how many got jobs—even in unrelated fields. Find out how many jobs were found through the placement office and how many students found them independently. Even if the school does not have a job placement service, you should be able to find out what percentage of graduating students find jobs in the computer industry. Try the recruitment office or office of alumni affairs for more information.

Does the School Offer Internships?

An internship is a source of experience and potential employment. It is an excellent opportunity for any student. In an internship, a student works in a company for a short time—often one to three months—to complete a predefined project or task.

The students are sometimes (but not always) paid a salary, which is usually low. Internships are valuable because they offer on-the-job experience, a chance to create portfolio pieces, and opportunities to network with other people in the field. If you perform well in an internship, chances are, you'll be hired by that company in a full-time position once your education and internship are completed.

So, in addition to considering an internship to be a learning experience, also think of it as an in-person audition for the job you'd eventually like to land. Find out if any of your prospective programs or schools have internships with companies in the area.

DESCRIPTIONS OF THE MAJOR TYPES OF TRAINING

There are many types of training available, ranging in length from a single day to several years. The two primary types of training are certification and degree, but there are many variables within these two categories.

Certification is a very specific task or tool training, generally given by a specialized business or a vendor who makes a product. Examples of certification are the training programs that you can take from Microsoft. As you probably know, Microsoft is a software design company, and the education you receive from them, obviously, specializes in their products. You can receive certification from vendors on one product or on an entire product line. You can receive certification in one day or in a course that could take up to a year or two.

A degree, on the other hand, is more of a general education based on concepts rather than specific technologies. You earn a degree from an accredited educational institute such as a university. Most schools offer several levels of degrees:

▶ Associate Degree—two years of study
▶ Bachelor's Degree—four years of study
▶ Master's Degree—six years of study

Type of Education	Description	Typical Time	Where to Get the Training
Course Certification	A class that focuses on one piece of software or one technology	Ranging from ½ day to 6 months	Temporary agencies Vendors (the companies that make hardware or software or other technologies)
Program Certification Degree	A series of classes that give an overview of a field General studies (arts, humanities, science, and so on) Specialized studies (computer science, mathematics, and so on)	1–2 years 2 years (AA plus degree) 4 years (BA/BS degree) 6 years (MA/MS degree)	Vocational schools Proprietary schools Colleges and universities

A SAMPLE WEBMASTER CURRICULUM

Techies.com (877-369-2214/www.techies.com) offers classroom and online-based training programs (distance learning) with a complete curriculum for becoming a qualified webmaster. The following is a summary of courses offered through this training program. Based on these course titles, you'll get a general idea of what's required these days to become a qualified webmaster with the skills in demand by today's top employers.

Getting Started

► Getting Started: How to Take a Course

CGI Perl Series

► CGI/Perl: 1 Getting Familiar with Forms
► CGI/Perl: 2 Building Programs
► CGI/Perl: 3 Web Applications
► CGI/Perl: 4 Interacting with Databases

Dynamic HTML Series

- ▶ Dynamic HTML: 1 DHTML and Style Sheets
- ▶ Dynamic HTML: 2 Using Javascript
- ▶ Dynamic HTML: 3 Objects and Events
- ▶ Dynamic HTML: 4 Styles and Content

E-Commerce Series

- ▶ E-Commerce: 1 Your E-Business
- ▶ E-Commerce: 2 Getting Started
- ▶ E-Commerce: 3 Influences on E-Commerce
- ▶ E-Commerce: 4 Killer Apps

FrontPage

- ▶ FrontPage 2000: Creating a webSite

GUI Design Series

- ▶ GUI Design: 1 Planning an Interface
- ▶ GUI Design: 2 Developing an Interface
- ▶ GUI Design: 3 Designing Screen Elements

HTML Series

- ▶ HTML: 1 Start Creating Your Own Web Pages
- ▶ HTML: 2 Creating High Quality Web Graphics
- ▶ HTML: 3 Layout and Design for Your Web Pages
- ▶ HTML: 4 Making Your Web Pages Interactive
- ▶ HTML: 5 Start Using JavaScript
- ▶ HTML: 6 Using JavaScript for Interactivity
- ▶ HTML: 7 Using Advanced JavaScript

JAVA 1.1 Series

- ▶ Java 1.1:1 Writing Java Programs
- ▶ Java 1.1:2 Java Programming Basics
- ▶ Java 1.1:3 Using Objects and Arrays
- ▶ Java 1.1:4 Creating Java Applets

▶ Java 1.1:5 Graphics and User Events
▶ Java 1.1:6 Putting Your Skills to Work

JAVA 1.2 Series

▶ Java 1.2:1 Writing Java Programs
▶ Java 1.2:2 Java Programming Basics
▶ Java 1.2:3 Using Objects and Arrays
▶ Java 1.2:4 Creating Java Applets
▶ Java 1.2:5 Graphics and User Events
▶ Java 1.2:6 Putting Your Skills to Work

Photoshop Series

▶ Photoshop: 1 Managing Graphics Files
▶ Photoshop: 2 Colors, Brushes, and Printing
▶ Photoshop: 3 Selecting and Retouching
▶ Photoshop: 4 Text, Fills, and Actions
▶ Photoshop: 5 Using Layers and Plug-Ins
▶ Photoshop: 6 Manipulating Images

Visual InterDev 6 Series

▶ Visual InterDev 6:1 Learning the Basics
▶ Visual InterDev 6:2 Using HTML
▶ Visual InterDev 6:3 Dynamic Content
▶ Visual InterDev 6:4 Objects and Databases
▶ Visual InterDev 6:5 Database Interaction
▶ Visual InterDev 6:6 Active Server Pages
▶ Visual InterDev 6:7 Controls and Scripts
▶ Visual InterDev 6:8 Testing and Debugging
▶ Visual InterDev 6:9 Management and Design

XML Series

▶ XML: 1 Viewing and Understanding XML
▶ XML: 2 Creating a Basic Document
▶ XML: 3 Building DTDs & Checking Documents

ACADEMIC- AND VENDOR-AFFILIATED TRAINING PROGRAMS

You can receive academic training through an accredited school, college, or university; this type of training provides you with a broad range of information about many elements of computers made by many different vendors.

This book contains information about two-year degrees—generally called associate degrees—and vendor training—generally called certification. Vendor certification provides intense training on all the products made by one company (such as Microsoft or Macromedia). Some academic programs also provide vendor training as a part of their degree program. Because computer technology is growing, the opportunities for training are increasing rapidly.

ACADEMIC COMPUTER TRAINING PROGRAMS

Because IT is still a relatively new field, most schools have their own naming conventions for programs. There are no universal terms used to name academic computer programs that relate to the Internet or the World Wide Web.

You rarely will find a program called webmaster, but there are a lot of closely related titles. Most programs offer essentially the same information—you will find many similar courses even under different program titles.

The best approach is to contact schools and ask for a catalog of their courses related to the IT (Internet/World Wide Web) field. Keep in mind, career paths and training programs are available for things like Web design, e-commerce, online security, computer animation, and networking. Call the schools that interest you and speak to an admissions counselor for more detailed information.

On the next page are two samples of academic training schools that have branches across the nation and that offer training for information technology professionals and webmasters.

DeVry Technical Institute

DeVry provides academic programs that unite education, technology, and business. The school offers two different programs for training computer technicians: Computer Information Systems and Electronics Technician. You can register for classes or get more information online at www.devry.com.

To be admitted to any DeVry program, you must:

▶ interview with a DeVry admission representative
▶ complete an application for admission
▶ be at least 17 years old on the first day of classes
▶ be a high school graduate, hold a GED certificate, or have a degree from an approved postsecondary institution
▶ provide an official transcript—or equivalent documentation—of your high school or college grade point average (GPA) and graduation date by the end of the first semester
▶ demonstrate proficiency in basic college-level skills

For your interview, you will meet with a campus- or field-based DeVry representative, who will provide you with information on programs, start dates, part-time work, student housing, and graduates' employment opportunities.

ITT Technical Institute

ITT Technical Institute (www.itt-tech.edu) provides education, technology, and business programs. It offers training for computer information professionals and webmasters in its Electronics Technician program.

To qualify for admission at ITT Technical Institute, an individual must:

▶ have a high school diploma, GED, or equivalent
▶ meet with a representative of ITT Tech
▶ pass an admissions exam
▶ arrange a time to tour the school
▶ pay the application fee

Courses are designed to help students prepare for career opportunities in various fields involving technology. ITT Technical Institute programs blend traditional academic content with applied learning concepts. A significant portion of course work is devoted to practical study in a lab environment.

Students can attend classes year-round and complete bachelor's degree programs in as few as three years. With classes typically available in the morning, afternoon and evening, students have the flexibility to pursue part-time employment opportunities.

ITT Technical Institute offers the following associates and bachelor's degree programs:

Associate's Degree Programs
- Electronics Engineering Technology
- Computer and Electronics Engineering Technology
- Computer-Aided Drafting Technology
- Computer-Aided Drafting & Design Technology
- Computer Drafting and Design
- Computer Network Systems Technology
- Information Technology—Computer Network Systems
- Information Technology—Multimedia
- Information Technology—Software Applications & Programming
- Information Technology—Web Development
- Chemical Technology
- Business Technology and Administration
- Tool Engineering Technology
- Heating, Air Conditioning & Refrigeration

Bachelor's Degree Programs
- Electronics Engineering Technology
- Computer Visualization Technology
- Automated Manufacturing Technology
- Industrial Design
- Telecommunications Engineering Technology

TIPS ON APPLYING TO ACADEMIC PROGRAMS

▶ Apply as early as you can. You'll need to fill out an application and submit official high school or GED transcripts and any copies of SAT, ACT, or other test scores used for admission. If you haven't taken these, you may have to before you can be admitted. Call the school and find out when the next programs start, when the application deadline is, and then apply at least a month or two prior to the deadline to make sure you complete all the requirements before the program starts.

▶ You may receive a prewritten request for transcripts from the admissions office when you get your application. Make sure you respond promptly so you don't hold up the admissions process.

▶ Make an appointment as soon as possible to take placement tests if they are required.

▶ Pay your fees before the deadline. Enrollment is not complete each quarter or semester until you have paid all fees by the date specified on the registration form. If fees are not paid by the deadline, your classes may be canceled. If you are going to receive financial aid, apply as early as you can.

▶ Find out if you must pass a physical or have any other medical history forms on file for the school you choose.

HOW TO MAKE THE MOST OF YOUR TRAINING PROGRAM

Simply signing up for a training program is step one. It's important that once you begin expanding your knowledge base and skill set that you get the most out of the education available to you. Here are some tips:

Choose Your Electives Carefully

The IT industry is still new, so you may or may not find a comprehensive training program titled *Webmaster*. Instead you will probably find programs with names like *Computer Science, Systems Engineer, Information Technology, Web*

Development, or *Information Science*. People with these degrees will get jobs as database administrators, network engineers, webmasters—just about any position available in the computer field.

So how can you adequately prepare yourself to become a webmaster? Even with different names, most of these programs include the same basic classes. That's why the same degree can be applied to so many different jobs. The thing that will make you stand out as a webmaster is your choice of electives. In most programs, about half the classes that you must take are already set, but then you get to choose from a pool of classes for the other half.

Choose your electives carefully. Some of the areas in which you might want to pursue classes include:

▶ web programming languages
▶ multimedia
▶ web site design
▶ e-commerce
▶ streaming media
▶ online security
▶ electronic publishing
▶ wireless communication
▶ web hardware
▶ software and networking

Get Hands-on Experience

Your training program probably has a technology lab available for student use. Take every opportunity to use the lab. If you have servers available, experiment with the hardware if permitted. Know how to take the server apart and understand how all the parts function. Also become familiar with installing and upgrading server software.

The lab will also probably have computers with many types of hardware and software. Become familiar with all the available hardware platforms in the lab, such as PC, Mac, and Unix. It's also critical that you become familiar with the popular operating systems and Web browsers in use by Web surfers in corporate America, at home, and throughout the world.

Take the time to learn many different software packages since you can't predict what kind of software your new employer will own. Make sure that you are familiar with at least two different e-mail packages, small databases, and Web page development packages. The lab is also a great opportunity for you to explore several different programming languages.

Take Notes in Class

Very few of us are gifted with a memory that allows us to retain all the information that bombards us throughout the day. And even fewer of us are gifted with a lightning-quick hand that can write down everything that is said in a classroom. So it is essential to your success in a training course that you use an effective note-taking method to help you learn and remember key information.

Here are some tips:

Traditional Outline

The traditional outline method typically mirrors the way that most teachers will lecture. Concepts (broad ideas) are furthest out in the left-hand margin, marked by roman numerals (I, II, III, etc.); the ideas and details that expand the concept are marked first by capital letters (A, B, C, etc.); then Arabic numbers (1, 2, 3, etc.); then lowercase letters (a, b, c, etc.). Increase the indent with each level of detail.

You don't have to get all the lettering and numbering perfect. The important part of this method is to understand and accurately record the relationships between the ideas (example: Idea *A* is a subset of that Idea *I*).

I. How to Make the Most of Your Training Program
   A. Taking Notes
      1. Outline
      2. Shorthand
   B. Studying for Exams

II. Finding the Training You Need

Invent Your Own Shorthand

Writing down every word in a lecture is virtually impossible. Don't even attempt this with a laptop, even if your typing skills are top-notch; you'll be miserable trying to condense and organize the material after class. You'll need to invent ways to abbreviate words. Constantly writing out *computer* and *because* and *training* is just silly and your wrist will protest. Just writing *bc* is sufficient for *because*. So many words end with *-ing*, why not just add *-g*? The common ending *-tion* can become *-tn*.

Drop as many vowels as possible without forgetting the meaning of the word. Therefore (and by the way, remember from science class that *therefore* is a triangle of dots?), *training* can easily become *trng*. Use acronyms (the first letter of each word) for key terms that are repeated over and over. Do you know how many times I could write *w.m.* while you're spelling out *webmaster?*

You rarely need to write complete sentences. The meat of a sentence is its noun and verb—skip all the extra words (*the*, *it*, and so on.). If you haven't tried it before, creating your own shorthand is going to take trial and error, just like any other note-taking method. Experiment with abbreviations while taking down information over the phone. Try recording a conversation with friends—even challenge everyone in the group to try it, and see who gets the most accurate information. Remember, it's not important that someone else understands your notes, only that *you* understand them.

Review Your Notes

Look over your notes as soon as possible after class—at least within 12 hours. Fill in any missing information that you still remember; cross out what obviously became unimportant by the time the class was done. Mark key points with a highlighter. Make sure each set of notes is clearly titled with date, course title, teacher's name, and overall theme.

Studying for Exams

Most of the time, studying in a group or with your significant other is *not* a good idea. Human nature has a way of reverting to socializing rather than studying. Additionally, if you've perfected your note-taking skills, your friends might not understand the information you've taken in your personal notes anyway. Save your study time for weeknights and save your friends for weekends; that's how the work-a-day world is going to be, so you might as well get used to it. You'll find that this is the most relaxing set-up of your time in the long run, even if it feels painful in the middle of the week. And it will also prevent the infamous "cram for the exam." Pulling an all-nighter is *not* your red badge of courage in education. Studies show that you will study less effectively and perform worse on the test when you are tired than when you are well rested and alert.

So, set up a reasonably neat study area and make sure:

- ▶ your lighting is good
- ▶ you have plenty of pens, pencils, Post-it™ notes, and highlighters
- ▶ your telephone isn't going to ring with a tempting offer to blow off your study plans
- ▶ you have a comfortable chair and posture
- ▶ if you prefer listening to music while you study, that you're not going to be distracted by song lyrics or the awesome bass
- ▶ you have access to a computer that's connected to the Internet. You can use this as a powerful tool for researching as well as practicing the hands-on skills you've learned

Ask your instructor what the format of the exam is going to be: essay, multiple choice, hands-on, or one of the many other methods of testing. You probably won't take many essay exams in your course work; more likely you will encounter a lot of multiple-choice and lab (hands-on) tests.

Networking with Other Students

Observe who is in more than one of your classes; they probably have some similar goals and interests. It would be a good idea to compare with them what their course of study is and what they plan for the near future when training is complete. Note announcements of get-togethers that are organized by major field of study, and attend with a friendly attitude. This will help you get to know students who are in the same boat as you, even if you didn't notice them before. On a more focused social note, get involved in student organizations on campus just for the fun of doing something different and broadening your horizons.

Getting to Know Your Instructors

It is important to have peers for moral support and fun, but it's just as important to get to know your instructors. Being just a number to them will do you no more good than taking a correspondence course. When they know you are flesh and blood—with a brain—your chance of learning more from their course increases.

You can approach them with questions that are specific to your field of study or just too time-consuming to ask in class. You will discover that professors and instructors are human too. They're not just robotic dispensers of knowledge. As soon as you've met one or two times in the classroom, find out your instructors' office hours. Make a point to drop by the office at least twice a month, even if it's just to chat about how things are going for you. Look for notices from student organizations announcing special social times to gather with instructors.

MAKING THE MOST OF YOUR CAREER PLACEMENT/ COUNSELING OFFICE

Just think, there are squadrons of people out there who have made it their job to run career placement and counseling offices just for you. Take advantage of all their available services. Make the office one of the first places you visit when you set foot on campus, and include it on your list as you're doing rounds to the instructors' offices.

Observe the posters and notices decorating the walls. Ask a lot of general questions initially to get a feel for the office; then try to ask one person your specific questions. This will prevent you from becoming just a number—by getting to know one particular person you are using the same strategy you used in getting to know your instructors. If one staff person takes an interest in your situation, they will be able to give you more personalized help and more detailed information.

Not every placement office works in exactly the same way. Get to know the details of how your school's office works. Most offices participate in career fairs and distribute candidate position lists. Career fairs are a great opportunity to learn more about companies in the field and trends in the marketplace, get experience interviewing, and find a job.

While the Career Placement/Counseling Office is a good place to start your job search efforts, one of the most powerful job search tools available to you is the Internet. After all, doesn't it make sense that people who are instrumental in creating and maintaining the Internet and World Wide Web would use this medium as a recruiting tool? Be sure to visit some of the many career-related websites—some of which are dedicated exclusively to people looking to land a job in the computer field. One of the very best career-related websites is The Monster Board (www.monster.com). When it comes to finding jobs in the computer field, ZDNet Careers (http://techies.zdnet.com) and Techies.com (www.techies.com) are excellent starting points.

THE INSIDE TRACK

Who: Alex Spinelli

What: Chief Technology Officer

Where: ComedyCentral.com

INSIDER'S STORY

My father was a software developer for Manufacturers Hanover Trust, so there were always computers in my house when I was growing up. I was used to playing with them, so computers never intimidated me. It was natural for me to use them—but I wasn't a "computer geek" back then.

In college I studied criminal justice and biology. When I was 19 or 20, I got an after-school job at Prodigy. That gave me a taste of the Internet, and I was blown away by the capacity for people to communicate on such a large scale.

I soon found out that I could make a lot of money and have a lot of fun building websites, so I left school three classes before graduation and went to work for a Web shop in Manhattan, where I built the first Reuters website. It was a fun new industry, and within two months I was building C and C++ applications. It came very naturally to me.

I have an interesting role in my current job. I have three basic responsibilities. The first is to develop technical strategies—How can we do this? Why is it the right idea? Is it feasible? We combine TV with interactive technologies, and I'm basically the new media technological consultant to the company at large. I also act as the software development manager and senior developer, and do a lot of infrastructure-based work, which involves managing the construction of the Network Operations Center.

INSIDER'S ADVICE

I'm a big proponent of people moving into this industry. My advice is to study the basics. Be sure to take as many additional courses as possible related to current technologies. Make a habit of constantly keeping up with new technologies. This medium is constantly changing; in three months, your four-year degree can become obsolete. I've been disappointed in the quality of undergraduate computer science programs, because the programs are slow to change; companies need people who understand *the* current technology. So, make a commitment to lifelong learning and recertification courses—you'll always need them. My advice: read a lot and ask plenty of questions.

By the way, my parents are still asking when I'm going to finish those last three classes. . . .

CHAPTER three

DIRECTORY OF TRAINING PROGRAMS AND FINANCIAL AID: DISCOVERING THE POSSIBILITIES

BEFORE YOU can begin your career as a webmaster or information technology (IT) professional, you must acquire what every employer is looking for—the necessary qualifications. Depending on what type of career path you're looking to pursue, this could mean obtaining anything from a post graduate degree, graduate degree, a four-year college degree, a high school diploma, plus one or more certifications (such as the internationally recognized Certified Internet Webmaster certification that's discussed later in this chapter).

Once you determine what level of education, skills training, and core knowledge base you need, this chapter will help you determine the best way of acquiring that training, taking into account your time constraints, budget, and how you as an individual prefer to be taught.

THE UNITED STATES Department of Labor estimates that over half of U.S. workers will require some type of IT skills training by 2002. Now that you've decided to get into a training program, you need to know what options are available near you. This chapter contains information about four main categories of training:

▶ academic programs offered by colleges and universities
▶ training programs offered by technical schools
▶ classroom-based, vendor-affiliated programs (including Microsoft)
▶ online and distance learning programs

NOTE: The specific schools and training programs included in this chapter are not endorsed or recommended by LearningExpress or the author, and not all training options that are available are listed here due to space limitations.

Conducting research on the Web is an excellent way of discovering various types of training opportunities in your city or geographic area. On any search engine (such as Yahoo.com or Google.com), use a search phrase such as "Certified Internet Webmaster," "webmaster training," or "Web Page Design Training" to find additional resources. You can also look in Appendix B of this book for additional resources, both print and online.

One online resource you'll find is The World Organization of Webmasters (WOW)'s website (www.joinwow.org). This is a professional organization with thousands of members and affiliates worldwide.

With the projected growth of website addresses growing from about 10 million today to 25 million by the year 2002, there is obviously a huge increase in demand for qualified webmasters. To meet this demand, WOW offers several options for aspiring and practicing webmasters to study topics identified as industry standard skills for certified web professionals. If you are looking for a complete Web certification program or one that can be adapted to fit existing curriculum, WOW can help meet your needs.

How Much Are You Worth as a Webmaster?

According to a 1999 ComputerWorld survey, in 1998, starting salaries for webmasters averaged about $49,400. Webmaster salaries jumped more than 11% to $53,000 in 1999. Some companies also offer cash bonuses, stock options, and higher salaries. These days, it's common for a webmaster at a medium-to-large sized company to earn at least $80,000 per year, plus receive a full benefits package.

As you begin to evaluate training programs, think carefully about what skills, knowledge, and training you actually need. For example, the webmaster career track can be divided into several areas of expertise, including: site design, application development, enterprise development, server administration, internetworking, security, and e-commerce.

According to WOW, "The following areas have been identified by indus try experts as standards to be achieved by various web professionals. Working with our Education Alliance partners worldwide, WOW offers the Certified Professional Webmaster Program in a variety of formats including traditional instruction, online instruction, independent study, and a hybrid method which includes elements of all three methods."

If you're starting from scratch and hope to break into the information technologies field and ultimately become a highly paid webmaster, The World Organization of Webmasters recommends pursuing one or more of the following certifications:

▶ WOW Certified Small Business Webmaster (CSBW)—Certified Small Business Webmasters are generalists or entrepreneurs interested in designing, building, and overseeing websites for small companies or personal business as the Web manager or project manager.

▶ WOW Certified Professional Webmaster (CPW)—Webmasters are practitioners of Web communication. They are responsible for all aspects of an organization's Web presence, including Web content development, technical operations, and business management.

▶ WOW Certified Web Graphics Designer (CGD)—Web Graphic Designers are masters of the visual arts and create the images and designs that capture and keep visitors' interest. They present aesthetically pleasing designs with minimal visitor hardware and plug-in requirements.

▶ WOW Certified Web Developer (CWD)—Web Developers are proficient at creating website interactivity. They use database tools and custom applications to prepare the site for dynamic presentation of content to the visitor.

▶ WOW Certified Web Administrator (CWA)—Web Administrators are responsible for the hardware and software supporting Internet communication. These technology professionals possess a strong understanding of servers, routers, security, network management, and systems maintenance.

▶ WOW Certified Internet Security Specialist (CSS)—Internet Security Specialists build and maintain data and communication structures providing for security of data, including databases, websites, files, and e-commerce transactions.

▶ WOW Certified E-Commerce and Marketing Specialist (CEMS)—
Web Marketers develop and execute Web marketing and e-commerce
strategies and operations. Web Marketers understand customer and
organizational needs and define the goals and objectives for the site.

As you can see, there are ranges of highly specialized skills that are required
for today's most successful webmasters to possess. Having any one of the
above certifications (or equivalent skills) will be enough to land you a job, but
being a specialist in several areas will definitely set you apart from other job
applicants and make you more desirable among high-paying employers looking to fill the most exciting jobs.

THE CERTIFIED INTERNET WEBMASTER CERTIFICATION

Another source of online training is PRM Training (www.prmtraining.com),
which offers several methods for obtaining a Certified Internet Webmaster
certification. This certification has quickly become the industry standard for
Internet certifications, and establishes an individual as an expert in Internet
technologies.

According to PRM Training, "As with any technical industry or product,
the Internet industry needed a way to validate the credentials and performance of Internet-related job candidates. CIW accomplishes this candidate
validation and much, much more."

This certification is very much like any of the Microsoft certification programs. It offers structured, reliable evidence of Internet skills competency.
Some of the professional benefits of obtaining the CIW certification include:

▶ objective validation of critical Internet skills
▶ verification tool for employers, allowing them to distinguish among candidates for hiring and promotion purposes
▶ an industry-wide, internationally accepted credential attesting to the mas-
tery of important skills required by webmasters in today's business world
▶ CIW is recognized as a leading industry standard by several independent Web professional associations, organizations, and corporations, and

is quickly becoming the certification and education standard in the Internet industry

The CIW program is:

▶ accredited by the Association of Internet Professionals (AIP)— www.association.org
▶ endorsed by the International Webmasters Association (IWA)— www.iwanet.org
▶ incorporated into IBM's global education offerings to all external education and enterprise customers
▶ integrated into Intel's training and certification program

The first step toward CIW certification is the CIW Foundations series. This provides a handful of introductory courses necessary for anyone looking to enter the webmaster or IT field. After successful completion of the Foundations exam, candidates are awarded a CIW Associate certification.

After achieving CIW Associate status, candidates can choose from three Master CIW certification tracks. Candidates who pass the CIW Foundations can earn the CIW Professional designation upon passing any CIW job role series exam. The Master CIW Designer certification is the highest level of certification for designers and webmasters. To earn the Master CIW Designer, the candidate must have passed the Foundations exam, the Site Designer exam, and the e-commerce exam.

People who should consider pursuing the Master CIW Designer certification include: Web authors, marketing and communications professionals, PR professionals, webmasters, graphic designers, desktop designers, technical writers, library scientists, network server administrators, firewall administrators, systems administrators, application developers, and IT security officers.

Obtaining the CIW certification is definitely an excellent starting strategy for anyone interested in becoming a webmaster or working in the IT field. Knowing that you want to earn this certification is step one. Step two is to actually obtain the necessary training, followed by acquiring hands-on experience.

For more information about this certification, the following are some websites that offer additional training options and information:

▶ www.ciwcertified.com

▶ www-3.ibm.com/services/learning/spotlight/ciw.html

▶ www.nextechtraining.com/training/certifications.php3

▶ http://209.207.167.177/bookstore/booksciw.html

▶ www.nhboston.com/courses/ciw/ciwcert.htm

▶ www.cce.edcc.edu/cce/ccecatalog/CertWeb.html

▶ www.ccilearning.com/ciw.asp

▶ www.etflorida.com/ciw/ciwtmp.htm

WHAT TO CONSIDER WHEN CHOOSING A TRAINING PROGRAM

Before you can sign up for a training program and begin acquiring the skills and knowledge you need to land a job in the webmaster or IT field, you need to make several very important decisions and do research. Begin by determining what aspect of the computer field you want to work in. Even if you've already decided you want to be a webmaster, there are several specialty areas you can choose to focus on. Having a clearly defined goal in terms of the type of job you hope to land will make it easier to obtain the appropriate training in the least amount of time.

What type of job or career path would you like to pursue? For example, do you want to work in the computer industry itself, or hold a webmaster- or IT-related job in another industry? Are you interested in designing, building, and maintaining websites or computer networks? Would you prefer to become a programmer or create the content for Web pages? Are you more interested in tapping your artistic side and becoming a computer animator or graphic artist? Each type of job within the IT field requires different training.

In addition to reading this book, it's an excellent strategy to review the help wanted ads in your local newspaper and conduct online research, for example, to learn about the types of job opportunities out there, what's required to obtain one of those jobs, what they pay, and what the day-to-day responsibilities of the job will be.

Most important, once you determine what type of job or career path you want to pursue, you'll need to determine what additional education you'll need and the best way to go about obtaining the necessary training. If, for example, a four-year college degree, graduate degree or postgraduate degree (a bachelor's degree, master's degree, or some other specialized degree) is required, chances are you'll need to investigate accredited colleges and universities with two-, three-, or four-year degree programs in your area of interest.

If you determine that a high school diploma in conjunction with the completion of a specific certification program is what's required, you'll probably want to look at attending a technical school, vendor-affiliated training program, or participate in some type of distance learning program, based on the funds you have available and the amount of time you're willing to invest in your education. Some of the pros and cons of each type of training program are outlined in this chapter.

ACADEMIC PROGRAMS OFFERED BY COLLEGES AND UNIVERSITIES

For many high-level technical jobs, including many in the IT field, the core requirements include a college diploma—and in some cases a higher-level graduate degree. To obtain this level of education, a two-, four-, or six-year commitment is typically required, as is enrollment in a traditional college or university.

If you want to enter into the IT field to ultimately become a webmaster, it's important to select a college or university that will provide you with a well-rounded education, but that can also provide you with the specialized training you'll need. Through research based on the career path you hope to pursue, you should easily be able to determine what type of education you require. The next step is to find a school that can offer you that education in an environment you'll prosper in.

There are a wide range of colleges and universities in the United States. Some are small campuses in a suburban environment, while others offer no formal campus and are based in the heart of a major city. Some educational institutions have small classes—with a small student-to-teacher ratio—while others have well-known and nationally recognized professors, but offer very large classes taught in a seminar fashion.

Some schools have on-campus housing and classes during the day, while others offer evening and weekend classes for students who live at home and work during the day. While the curriculum taught to prepare students for specific occupations may be somewhat standard, how this information is taught will vary greatly from institution to institution.

In general, the college experience involves attending regularly scheduled classes and seminars, doing hands-on work in computer labs, completing individual and group projects, completing homework assignments, and, ultimately, passing exams. For each course you complete you'll earn college credit. By completing the core requirements and earning enough credits, you'll graduate with a degree over a two- or four-year period, depending on the program. In a traditional college environment, classroom attendance and lab work are often mandatory.

Choosing the right college or university to attend will require considerable research on your part. You'll need to choose schools that meet your requirements, schedule an in-person tour of the school, schedule a meeting with someone from the admissions department for an interview, and then formally apply for admission.

There are literally thousands of colleges and universities in the United States. Some are considered highly respected Ivy League colleges or universities, while others are classified as state schools or private colleges/universities. When it comes to technology, few schools are more respected than MIT (Massachusetts Institute of Technology). According to a ranking done by US News Online, some other top schools for IT are California Institute of Technology, Stanford University, University of California at Berkeley, Georgia Institute of Technology, and Cornell University.

Once you have a general career path you're interested in pursuing, contact the career counselor at your high school, community college, or library for advice on choosing the best college to meet your needs. The reference section of any bookstore will also have a selection of directories that describe colleges and universities.

Using the Internet, there are an abundance of free resources online that can help you find the best possible college or university that offers the type of computer training you're interested in. For example, Thomson Learning's

Peterson's website (www.Petersons.com) offers detailed information about thousands of colleges and universities, graduate programs, IT programs, adult/distance learning programs, training and executive education programs, and private schools. The area of this website called "IT Channel" is of particular interest to those looking to pursue a career in the information technologies or webmaster field.

An extremely useful feature of the Peterson's website is a searchable database of two-year IT programs in the United States. By selecting an area of interest, followed by geographic location, the database will provide you with a listing of schools that are appropriate to your needs. This company also publishes a book, *Peterson's Handbook for College Admissions* by Thomas C. Hayden that offers detailed advice on how to choose a college. Another related website that offers a useful resource to people researching colleges can be found by pointing your Web browser to www.collegecenter.com.

To pursue any type of college-level courses, a high school diploma or GED is required. The benefit of attending an accredited college or university is that you will graduate with a degree and a diploma that will be recognized in any industry in which you choose to work. It is likely that you will have a well-rounded education, as well as specialized computer-related skills and knowledge.

For some candidates, the main issues with attending a two- or four-year college or university is the significant expense and time commitment involved. However, with the help of scholarships, student loans, and family support, many high school students graduate and continue directly into college before entering the job market. Obtaining as much education and training as possible is always an excellent long-term career strategy, but it's a path that not everyone can take.

Later in this chapter, other, often cheaper, degree options will be presented—such as earning a college or graduate degree by participating in a distance learning program. This means that you can obtain the education and training you need, at your own pace, and around your own schedule.

TRAINING PROGRAMS OFFERED BY TECHNICAL SCHOOLS

Instead of offering a well-rounded education combined with specialized computer courses, technical schools generally offer only the specific courses and training needed to obtain a specific degree or certification. Depending on the type of degree or certification you choose to pursue, it could take you anywhere from several months to several years to complete the program. Fortunately, classes are offered during the day, in the evening, and/or on weekends to accommodate the schedules of students who are also often employed.

While students are required to attend classes, perform hands-on work in labs, complete projects, and pass exams, most technical schools offer a different learning environment than a traditional college or university. The tuition tends to be cheaper, but the ultimate degree or certification earned will be widely accepted in the webmaster or IT job markets.

Another benefit of technical schools is that each typically offers a variety of different certification or degree programs, plus a broad range of computer or IT-related classes. A vendor-affiliated training center might not offer the same range of course work. Consider your choice carefully because when it comes to designing, building, and maintaining websites of any kind, it is vital to be able to utilize the latest and most popular technologies, tools, and programming techniques that are available from a range of manufacturers. For example, becoming proficient at using Microsoft FrontPage 2000 will help you develop basic Web pages, but to add animation, you'll need to utilize a program or a programming language such as Macromedia's Flash. Different tools are then used to incorporate streaming audio or video into a website. Thus, becoming a competent webmaster will mean becoming familiar with a range of development tools, technologies, and programming languages.

VENDOR-AFFILIATED TRAINING PROGRAMS

No matter where you live, chances are there is a vendor-affiliated training program offered in your area. These training centers are licensed or authorized to teach curriculums developed by a specific software or hardware manufacturer, or by professional organizations, such as Microsoft, Intel, IBM, The World Organization of Webmasters, The Association of Internet Professionals, or the International Webmasters Association.

As you discovered in Chapter 2, companies like Microsoft have developed standardized training programs for their key products, networks, and operating systems, and have contracted with independent training centers across the United States to offer this curriculum to students in order to prepare them for exams required to earn a specific certification.

If you want to become a Microsoft Certified Professional, for example, the first step is to visit the Microsoft training website (www.microsoft.com/trainingandservices) to learn more about what type of jobs this certification will prepare you for. You can also determine what training centers are available in your area.

According to Microsoft, "Microsoft Certified Solution Providers (MCSPs) are independent companies that can provide you with the highest levels of technical expertise, strategic thinking, and hands-on skills. MCSPs encompass a broad range of expertise and vendor affiliations and their real world perspective can help you prioritize and effectively deliver your technology solutions."

To become a Microsoft Certified Professional (MCP), for example, you must pass one or more Microsoft certification exams. Microsoft offers certifications focused on specific areas of expertise and ranges of job skills. Decide which certification—or certifications—is appropriate for you, based on your experience, skills, and interests.

Once you choose to pursue the certificate, programs with instructor-led, online, and self-paced (distance learning) training are available. Each of these options is designed to prepare students to pass certification exams that are administered at specific testing centers throughout the country.

The following two independent companies offer testing centers for Microsoft and a wide range of other vendor-affiliated certification programs. Additional information about these testing facilities can be obtained by contacting:

NCS—Virtual University Enterprises
Suite 300
11000 Prairie Lakes Drive
Eden Prairie, MN 55344-3857
Voice: 612-995-8800
www.vue.com

Sylvan Prometric
1000 Lancaster Street
Baltimore, MD 21203
410-843-8000
www.prometric.com

The advantages to participating in vendor-affiliated training programs are plentiful. For example, the actual time it takes to earn a certification will range from several weeks to several months, depending on your level of commitment and the speed at which you learn the material. Once you have the certification, you'll be qualified to fill jobs in that area. While the initial salary range might not be as high as someone with a college or graduate degree would receive, you will be qualified to fill a technical position that puts you in a higher-earning bracket than someone looking for an entry-level IT job who has no certification and minimal qualifications.

Furthermore, by obtaining a vendor-affiliated certification, you're obtaining training that is recognized and respected by employers. For example, with a Microsoft certification, companies that use Microsoft products know they're hiring someone who is qualified for the job. As a result, a greater number of job opportunities will be available to you if you possess the certification(s) employers are looking for.

The cost of participating in a vendor-affiliated certification program is also much less than pursuing a college education or degree with a technical school. Furthermore, most training centers offer classes designed to accommodate almost anyone's schedule. Plus, if you're already employed and looking to further both your education and your computer-related skills, you may find that your current employer will pay for this type of training.

As you'll quickly discover by visiting the website of a company such as Microsoft, independent-training centers are available across the United States. In many cases, even your local retail computer superstore can offer the training you require. For example, many CompUSA stores have fully equipped training centers and a broad range of training programs.

CompUSA's Authorized Advanced Technology Sites (www.compusa.com/training) present an expanded selection of high-tech courses. Authorized training is offered in an open enrollment format at various locations, and, if for any reason you are not fully satisfied with a class, you can retake it within one year.

DISTANCE LEARNING PROGRAMS

There are many reasons why someone might want to pursue their education through a distance learning program, and with recent advances in Internet technology—such as streaming audio and video on the Web—distance learning has been brought to an whole new level, making it easier to obtain a complete education from any desktop computer that's connected to the Internet. Distance learning is an extremely viable option for IT students—especially individuals who are holding down full-time jobs, have limited time in their daily schedules, or have financial limitations. These days, it's possible to earn a high school equivalency diploma (or GED), undergraduate degree, graduate degree, or almost any type of computer-related certification by participating in a distance learning program. You learn the same exact material as you would by participating in traditional classes; however, your education is done at home, at your own pace, through reading, participating in online courses, listening to audiocassettes, and/or watching videocassettes.

Assuming you pass the exams associated with the distance learning program, the end result and the degree or certification you earn is identical to what someone who attended a traditional educational institution would earn.

According to the U.S. Department of Education, the percentage of 25- to 34-year olds enrolled as college undergraduates increased by nearly one-third between 1972 and 1994. In the even shorter period between 1976 and 1994, the percentage of undergraduates age 35 and older increased by about one-third. As a result, there are numerous programs for students with non-traditional learning curves.

Distance study diploma programs have no residency requirements, allowing students to continue their studies from almost any location. Depending on the course of study, students need not be enrolled full time, and they usually have more flexible schedules for finishing their work.

Taking courses by distance study is often more challenging and time consuming than attending classes, especially for adults who have other obligations.

Success depends on an individual student's motivation. Students usually do reading assignments on their own, but completed written exercises are sent to an instructor for grading.

A list of some accredited high schools that offer diplomas by distance study is available free from the Distance Education and Training Council. Request a copy of the "*DETC*" *Directory of Accredited Institutions*" by calling 202-234-5100. Adult learners can also contact their local school system, community college, or university to learn about programs that are readily available. The following national organizations can also supply information.

American Council on Education
One Dupont Circle
Washington, DC 20036-1193
202-939-9300

Distance Education and Training Council
1601 18th Street, NW
Washington, DC 20009-2529
202-234-5100

National University Continuing Education Association
One Dupont Circle, Suite 615
Washington, DC 20036
202-659-3130

Many well-known and accredited colleges, universities, and technical/vocational schools now offer distance learning programs in the computer or IT field. For example, at the School of Information Technology, Kaplan College has built an online campus community that brings online learning directly to you.

The Commission on Institutions of Higher Education of the North Central Association of Colleges and Schools (NCA) accredits Kaplan Colleges. As an accredited academic institution of higher education, Kaplan College has been approved as a Microsoft Authorized Academic Training Program (AATP) institution and delivers technical training using Microsoft Official Curriculum and other authorized materials.

TAKING THE NEXT STEP: FINANCIAL AID AND SCHOLARSHIPS FOR THE TRAINING YOU NEED

By making the decision to pursue additional training and making yourself qualified for better, higher paying jobs in the computer field, you have made an extremely good decision that will open up new and exciting career paths for you in the future. This section explains how to determine your eligibility for financial aid, and will help you gather relevant information before you begin the financial aid process. There are many types of financial aid available, plus an even larger selection of scholarships for which you may be eligible. The lists of resources and acronyms provided in this chapter will help you along the financial aid path.

Getting Started

You will need a plan for financing your training. If you've already been in the workforce and plan to change careers, or if your parents have offered to pay for your education, perhaps you already have the money you'll need. There's no harm, however, in spending time investigating the financial aid and scholarship options available, even if you think you might not qualify.

Financial aid is available to cover the cost of education and training at several different types of schools—including vocational schools that offer short-term training programs. It's possible to qualify even if you're attending only part time. The financial aid you'll get may be less than that for longer, full-time programs, but it still can help you pay for a portion of your IT or webmaster certification training program. Also, if you're currently employed, be sure to contact your employer to determine if the company will cover some or all of your education or training.

Free Application for Federal Student Aid (FAFSA)

First of all, get a Free Application for Federal Student Aid (FAFSA) from your public library or financial aid office. You can also order it online at www.finaid.org/finaid.html, or call 800-4-FED-AID. Be aware that photo-copies of federal forms are not acceptable. The FAFSA determines your eligibility status for all grants and loans provided by federal or state govern-ments and certain college or institutional aid, so this is a mandatory first step in the financial aid process.

The U.S. government—as well as state governments—offers a wide range of scholarships and financial aid packages for civilians, plus special aid pro-grams for present and former military personnel. There are also attractive tax benefits associated with obtaining additional education or training. Aside from the government, there are many other options available, some of which are outlined at www.finaid.org/otheraid.

According to the government, anyone in the process of applying to school should complete the FAFSA form. "Many families mistakenly think they don't qualify for aid and prevent themselves from receiving financial aid by failing to apply for it. In addition, there are a few sources of aid, such as unsubsidized Stafford and PLUS loans, that are available regardless of need. The FAFSA form is free. There is no good excuse for not applying," explains one FAFSA brochure.

For more information, contact the Federal Student Aid Information Cen-ter (FSAIC) and ask for a free copy of *The Student Guide: Financial Aid from the U.S. Department of Education.* The toll free hotline (800-4-FED-AID) is run by the U.S. Department of Education to answer your questions about federal and state student aid programs and applications. You can also write to: Federal Stu-dent Aid Information Center, P.O. Box 84, Washington, DC 20044. The FAFSA website (www.fafsa.ed.gov) will help you obtain and complete the FAFSA form. To complete this form, you'll need the following information:

▶ records for income earned in the year prior to when you will start school. (You may also need records of your parent's income informa-tion.) For the 2001–2002 school year, you will need 2000 information.

▶ your Social Security card and driver's license

▶ W-2 forms or other records of income earned

▶ your (and your spouse's, if you are married) federal income tax return

▶ your parent's federal income tax return—if applicable to your situation

▶ records of other untaxed income received such as welfare benefits, Social Security benefits, Temporary Assistance for Needy Families (TANF), veteran's benefits, or military or clergy allowances

▶ current bank statements and records of stocks, bonds, and other investments

▶ business or farm records, if applicable

▶ your alien registration card if you are not a U.S. citizen

To complete the form online using FAFSA Express, go to: www.sfadownload. ed.gov/fafsa/fexpress.html. FAFSA Express makes applying online for financial aid, faster and easier. The process automatically checks electronic FAFSA data, resulting in fewer rejected applications.

Gathering Your Records

When you apply for financial aid, your answers to certain questions will determine whether you're considered dependent on your parents and must report their income and assets as well as your own, or whether you're independent and must report only your own income and assets (and those of your spouse if you're married).

If you are a dependent student, you will need financial information from your parents to fill out the FAFSA. You are considered an independent student if you meet any one of the following criteria:

▶ You are at least 24 years old.

▶ You are married.

▶ You have a dependent other than a spouse.

▶ You are a graduate student or professional student.

▶ You are a ward of the court or an orphan.

▶ You are a veteran of the U.S. Armed Forces.

Determining Your Eligibility

To receive financial aid from an accredited college or institution's student aid program, you must be a U.S. citizen or an eligible noncitizen with a Social Security number. Check with Immigration and Naturalization Service (INS)

if you are not a U.S. citizen and are unsure of your eligibility (800-375-5283 or www.ins.usdoj.gov/graphics/index.htm).

Eligibility is a very complicated matter, but it can be simplified to the following equation:

Your contribution + your parents' contribution = expected family contribution (EFC)

Student expense budget/cost of attendance (COA) — EFC = your financial need

The need analysis service or federal processor looks at the following if you are a dependent student:

▶ family assets, including savings, stocks and bonds, real estate investments, business/farm ownership, and trusts
▶ parents' ages and need for retirement income
▶ number of children and other dependents in the family household
▶ number of family members in college
▶ cost of attendance—also called student expense budget—which includes tuition/fees, books and supplies, room and board (living with parents, on or off campus), transportation, personal expenses, and special expenses, such as childcare

Types of Financial Aid

The two major types of financial aid are gift aid and self-help aid. Gift aid—a gift that does not need to be paid back—consists of grants and scholarships. Grants are awarded based on financial need, whereas scholarships are almost always awarded on academic merit or special characteristics—such as ethnic heritage, interests, parents' careers, or geographic location—rather than financial need. Also, they usually only apply to tuition and other educational expenses, but not living expenses.

Self-help aid consists of loans and student employment (also called work-study). There are many types of loans, all of which you have to repay with interest. Payment schedules and interest rates vary. You can arrange to work to help pay your school bills either on your own or in partnership with your school, taking into account your field of interest.

Gift aid and self-help aid are each available on four levels: federal, state, school, and private. You will encounter an amazing number of acronyms while applying for any type of federal financial aid. Refer to the acronym list at the end of this chapter for help. Also use the Internet as a supplemental source of information. A list of additional Internet addresses can be found in the Resources section at the end of this chapter.

Using any Internet search engine, such as Google (www.google.com) or Dogpile (www.dogpile.com), enter the search phrase "Financial Aid" to gain access to a wide selection of online-based resources relating to scholarships, loans, lending organizations, and financial planning. For example, eStudentLoan.com (www.estudentloan.com) is a searchable database of loans available to all types of potential full-time and part-time students. According to this service, there are five steps to consider before financing your education. These include:

1. Talking with the financial aid officers at your school. These are the best people to prepare you for your journey through the financial aid process.
2. Talking to your family. Have an in-depth discussion with your parents and/or family members about how they might play a role in financing your education. Will they lend you money? Will they cosign for loans? Will they borrow money for you?
3. Understanding the financial aid process. The more you know about the financial aid system, the better prepared you will be to pay for school.
4. Don't limit your options by automatically ruling out high-cost schools. The financial aid system works proportionally, making up the difference of what you can afford to pay and what your education costs.
5. Create a financial plan to pay for college. Do some research about which programs you can use to pay your way.

Loans: Federal, State, School, and Private

The following section outlines some of the loan types you can apply for to pay for your education or training. Keep in mind, this section discusses only some of your options. Through research and a bit of creativity, chances are you'll discover ways of paying for the education or training you need. If you're currently employed, don't neglect to contact your employer about paying for some or all of your education or training. Some employers will subsidize additional education or make low-interest loans available to employees.

Federal Loans

One online source of information about federal, state, and private loans and scholarships can be found at www.educaid.com or by calling 1-800-EDUCAID. Educaid is one of the top ten education lenders in the United States. Its mission is to provide "the knowledge that helps pay for college" and to help make education possible for more students and their families. Educaid, a division of First Union National Bank, has been providing education loans since 1984.

The Internet Student Loans Company (www.collegenet.com/about/index.html), American Student Financial Aid Services (www.edudotfunding.com), and The Federal College Student Loans Directory (www.college-student-loans.com) are also excellent online-based resources. To find additional resources on the Web, use any search engine and enter the search phrase or keyword "student loans."

Perkins Loans

The Perkins Loan (www.ed.gov/prog_info/SFA/StudentGuide/1999-0/perkins.html) is for students with acute financial need, so the interest rate is low (5% as of late 2000). You repay your school, which lends you the money with government funds. You can borrow up to $3,000 each year, up to a total of $15,000 over the course of your undergraduate study.

The school pays you directly by check or credits your account. You have nine months after you graduate—provided you were continuously enrolled at least half time—to begin repayment, with up to 10 years to pay off the entire loan. A Perkins Loan borrower is not charged any fees. However, if you skip a payment, make a late payment, or make less than a full payment, you may have to pay a late charge plus any collection costs. Late charges will continue until your payments are current.

Examples of Typical Payments for Perkins Loan Repayment

A borrower with a total loan amount of $3,000 will

▶ Have 119 monthly payments of $31.84 and a final payment of $28.90

▶ Pay $817.86 in interest charges

▶ Repay a total of $3,817.86

A borrower with a total loan amount of $5,000 will

▶ Have 119 monthly payments of $53.06 and a final payment of $49.26

▶ Pay $1,363.40 in interest charges

▶ Repay a total of $6,363.40

A borrower with a total loan amount of $15,000 will

▶ Have 119 monthly payments of $159.16 and a final payment of $150.81

▶ Pay $4,090.85 in interest charges

▶ Repay a total of $19,090.85

The Perkins Loan program is also available to graduate students. Graduate students can obtain up to $5,000 per year or $30,000 for the entire time enrolled—including Federal Perkins Loans you borrowed as an undergraduate.

Stafford Loans

Both subsidized and unsubsidized Federal Stafford Loans are available to students who need help paying for college. The financial aid office at your school will determine which loan you may be able to receive.

▶ Subsidized loans (the Federal government pays the interest) are awarded on a need basis—this is also called a Direct Stafford Loan.

▶ Unsubsidized loans (you pay the interest) are awarded on request. This is also called Federal Family Education Loan (FFEL) Stafford Loan. The unsubsidized Federal Stafford loan is available to all students regardless of income. Because this loan is not subsidized by the government, you are responsible for all interest that accrues while you are in school, in deferment or during your grace period. You may choose to make interest payments while in school or may defer—and accumulate—the interest until repayment.

These loans have many borrowing limits, depending on whether you get an unsubsidized or subsidized loan, which school year you're in, the length of your program, and whether you're independent or dependent. You can have both kinds of Stafford loans at the same time, but the total loaned at any time cannot exceed $23,000. The interest rate varies but will never exceed 8.25%. There is a six-month grace period after graduation before you must start repaying the loan.

The annual limits for subsidized Federal Stafford Loans are:

Year 1	Year 2	Year 3	Year 4	Year 5	Graduate/Professional
$2,625	$3,500	$5,500	$5,500	$5,500	$8,500

The combined annual limits for the subsidized and unsubsidized Federal Stafford Loans are:

Year in School	Dependent Student	Independent Student
1	$2,625	$6,625
2	$3,500	$7,500
3	$5,500	$10,500
4	$5,500	$10,500
5	$5,500	$10,500
Graduate/Professional	N/A	$18,500

If you're enrolled full time in courses that serve as prerequisites to a degree or certificate program, you're eligible for Stafford Loans up to these limits:

	Undergraduate	Graduate
Subsidized Stafford	$2,625	$5,500
Unsubsidized Stafford	$4,000	$5,000

In addition, according to Educaid, if you have a bachelor's degree and you're enrolled full time in a state teacher certification program, you're eligible for $5,500 in subsidized and $5,000 in unsubsidized Stafford Loan funds.

PLUS Loans (Loans for Parents)

Educaid reports, "To take out a Federal PLUS Loan, you must be the parent of a dependent child who is enrolled at an approved school at least half-time and is making satisfactory academic progress. You should have no adverse credit history. Federal PLUS loans are not based on parents' income."

It's possible to borrow up to the cost of education, minus other financial aid awarded. In this case, the cost of education includes: tuition and fees, room and board, books and supplies, transportation, and miscellaneous expenses.

PLUS Loans are made to your parents and they are responsible for repayment. They must have a good credit history; you must be their dependent and be enrolled at least half time.

The borrowing limit equals your cost of attendance (COA) minus all other financial aid you're receiving. The PLUS Loan has a variable interest rate based on the 91-day T-Bill + 3.1%, adjusted each July 1, with a cap of 9%. Effective July 1, 2000, PLUS Loans first disbursed on or after July 1, 1998, have an interest rate of 8.99%. The lender for these loans charges no fees; however, the borrower is responsible for two other fees. The U.S. Department of Education charges an origination fee of 3%, and the loan guarantor may charge up to 1% for a guarantee fee. Your parents must begin repayment while you're still in school. There is no grace period.

Consolidation Loans

This is an umbrella term for merging all your loans into one easy monthly payment. Details vary greatly, depending on your particular borrowing plans. Consolidation loans also can be arranged on the school and private levels.

State Loans

Many states have websites, but you can find the same information by contacting your state's department of education. You can qualify for state loans based on your residency, your parents' residency, or the location of the school you're attending.

School Loans

You can get information on these loans only through the financial aid office at the school of your choice. Quickly become acquainted with the financial aid administrators and stay in close touch. Their full-time job is to help you with your financial aid questions.

Private Loans
Check several banks, savings and loan institutions, and credit unions for loan programs. If you are dependent, consult your parents about their financial institutions and ask them to do some footwork for you in researching borrowing opportunities. Pay careful attention to interest rates and grace periods when applying for private loans.

Grants and Scholarships: Federal, State, School, and Private
This is the painless money—the kind you don't have to pay back. Again, don't assume you don't qualify simply because you think your finances are in pretty good shape, especially where scholarships are concerned. You won't know how much financial aid you qualify for unless you file the forms and get the process started.

Federal Grants and Scholarships

Pell Grants
This program is one of the largest and provides a foundation of financial aid upon which many students build. It is completely based on financial need. You can even be enrolled less than half time to qualify. If you already have a bachelor's degree, you can't receive a Pell Grant. You will not be considered for certain other sources of financial aid if you haven't first applied for a Pell Grant.

To apply for student financial aid from the federal government, including the Pell Grant, Perkins Loan, Stafford Loan, and work-study, you will need to submit the Free Application for Federal Student Aid (FAFSA) discussed earlier in this chapter. All state and many school student assistance programs also require the FAFSA.

Federal Supplemental Educational Opportunity Grants (FSEOG)
Priority consideration for FSEOG funds is given to students receiving Pell Grants because the FSEOG program is based on exceptional financial need.

The FSEOG differs from the Pell Grant in that it is not guaranteed that every student in need will receive one. Each school has only a certain amount of funds to distribute among all students with a financial need.

National Merit Scholarships
About 5,000 students each year receive this scholarship—based solely on academic performance in high school—from the National Merit Scholarship Corporation. If you are a high school senior with excellent grades and high scores on tests such as the ACT and SAT, this scholarship can be for you.

State Grants and Scholarships
State grants and scholarships may be specific to the state in which you are trained, the state in which you reside, or the state in which your parents reside—even if you plan to attend another school out of state. A handful of states have websites about state grants; these include California, Idaho, Kentucky, Illinois, and Tennessee. Not all state grants can be used to attend out-of-state schools; check with your state grant agency for details.

School Grants and Scholarships

You need to know which school you'll be attending to pursue a school grant or scholarship. Once you've overcome that hurdle, immediately talk to the financial aid administrator (FAA) to find out specific details about school-based grants. The financial aid office offers a wealth of information about all student aid programs, application requirements, eligibility, advice on financial planning and debt management, advice about applying for a student loan, and the associated interest rates and payment schedules. They can even help with short-term loans in a financial emergency. Check it out!

Private Grants and Scholarships

It is always worthwhile to look into religious organizations, businesses, labor unions, and community and professional groups for private grants and scholarships. You can find highly specific sources of financial aid in the private sector. For example, you can obtain a scholarship for being a certain gender in a certain field, of a particular ethnicity, an athlete, or a music lover. Places to look for help include local community organizations such as the Rotary Club, American Legion, 4H Club, chamber of commerce, PTA/PTSA, and Boy Scouts and Girl Scouts. Perhaps your parents' companies offer financial aid to children of employees. Check with the personnel office. Also check with your library for directories of professional, career, and trade associations in the computer industry that offer scholarships and loans—especially if you are specializing in a certain company's software or hardware. Read computer-related magazines. You never know what type of private aid you might dig up.

Work Study

Your school's student employment office is the place to head for more information about work-study. Work options include on- or off-campus; part time or almost full time; in the computer field or just to pay the bills; for money to repay student loans or to go directly toward educational expenses.

One advantage of working under Federal Work Study (FWS) is that your earnings are exempt from FICA taxes if you are enrolled full time and are working less than half time. You will be paid by the hour, at least minimum wage. For FWS, you must demonstrate financial need. The total hourly wages you earn cannot exceed your total FWS award. Your financial aid administrator (FAA) or the direct employer must consider your class schedule and your academic progress before assigning your job.

For more information about National Work Study programs, visit the Corporation for National Service website (www.cns.gov) and/or contact:

▶ **National Civilian Community Corps (NCCC)**—This AmeriCorps program is an 11-month residential national service program intended for 18-24 year-olds. Participants receive $4,725 for college tuition or to help repay education loan debt. Contact: National Civilian Community Corps, 1100 Vermont Avenue NW, Washington, DC 20525. Call: 800-94-ACORPS.
▶ **VISTA Volunteers in Service to America**—VISTA is part of ACTION, the federal domestic volunteer agency. This program offers

numerous benefits to college graduates with outstanding student loans. Contact: VISTA, Washington, DC 20525. Call: 800-424-8867.

AmeriCorps, the domestic Peace Corps, engages more than 40,000 Americans in intensive, results-driven service. Most AmeriCorps members are selected by and serve with local and national organizations like Habitat for Humanity, the American Red Cross, Big Brothers/Big Sisters, and Boys and Girls Clubs. This is one example of how you can earn money for your education through work-study. Throughout our nation, many schools are discovering the value of service learning through projects that link education and service, and at the forefront of this movement is Learn and Serve America (www.learnandserve.org). This organization helps support nearly one million students from kindergarten through college who are meeting community needs while improving their academic skills and learning the habits of good citizenship.

Filing Your Forms

Start investigating financial aid as soon as possible. The FAFSA can be filed any time between January 1 and June 30; however, the closer to January 1, the better. Do not file before January 1 of the year in which you want to obtain financial aid, or your application will be discarded. You will need federal and state income tax information, but even if you or your parents haven't filed yet, you can submit the FAFSA with estimated income tax information. You may wish to mail your application by certified mail. If you fill out the postcard included with the FAFSA, it will be returned to you to mark receipt of your FAFSA by the federal processor. Within four weeks after you mail the form, you should receive a Student Aid Report (SAR) detailing your eligibility. Your SAR will also be forwarded for Pell Grant evaluation and up to six schools of your choice. If more than four weeks go by and you don't get the SAR, call the federal processor at 319-337-5665 to find out what happened. You will be asked for your Social Security number and date of birth as verification.

Your application must be received by June 30 of the school year you want to attend. The Student Aid Report (SAR) must be at your school by August 31 or your last day of enrollment of that school year, whichever is earlier. Carefully meet any deadlines set by state, school, or private sources of financial aid. Your Financial Aid Administrator (FAA) should make these clear to you.

If all goes well, you will receive financial assistance to become a computer technician. If you get a loan, be sure you understand how the money will pay your bills—will it be paid directly to the school, deposited in your account, sent to you in check form? And just as important, be sure you understand how you are to pay back the loan. Most loans require no payment until you have completed your training. However, there are rules about staying enrolled, taking leaves of absence, grace periods after graduation, and so on. You need to investigate and take responsibility for loan repayment once you accept financial aid. Also talk to the financial aid office about spreading your payments over the school year rather than paying in a lump sum, and consolidating more than one loan into one payment.

Note that you have to reapply for financial aid every year that you are in school. Once you are started on financial aid, you should receive a renewal FAFSA by January 15 each year. Probably 75% of the information will remain the same from year to year, but you may need to report changes in your income, how many of your family members are in college, and your family size. Always have a copy of each year's FAFSA sent to your school's financial aid office.

Financial Aid Checklist

1. Explore your options as soon as possible after you've decided to begin a training program.
2. Find out what your school requires and what financial aid it offers.
3. Complete and mail the FAFSA as soon as possible after January 1.
4. Complete and mail other applications by the deadlines.
5. Gather loan application information and forms from your college financial aid office. You must forward the completed loan application to your financial aid office for processing. Remember to sign the loan application.
6. Carefully read all letters and notices from the school, the federal student aid processor, the need analysis service, and private scholarship organizations. Note whether financial aid will be sent before or after

you are notified about admission, and how exactly you will receive the money. Return all requested documents promptly.

7. Report any changes in your financial resources or expenses to your financial aid office so your award can be adjusted accordingly.

8. Reapply each year.

Maximize Your Eligibility for Loans and Scholarships

Loans and scholarships are often awarded based on someone's eligibility. Depending on the type of loan or scholarship you pursue, the eligibility requirements will be different. eStudentLoan.com (www.estudentloan.com/workshop.asp) offers the following tips and strategies for improving your eligibility when applying for loans and/or scholarships:

▶ Save money in the parent's name, not the student's name.

▶ Pay off consumer debt, such as credit card and auto loan balances.

▶ Parents considering going back to school should do so at the same time as their children. The more family members in school simultaneously, the more aid will be available to each.

▶ Spend student assets and income first, before other assets and income.

▶ If you believe that your family's financial circumstances are unusual, make an appointment with the financial aid administrator at your school to review your case. Sometimes the school will be able to adjust your financial aid package to compensate.

▶ Minimize capital gains.

▶ Do not withdraw money from your retirement fund to pay for school. If you must use this money, borrow from your retirement fund.

▶ Minimize educational debt.

▶ Ask grandparents to wait until the grandchild graduates before giving them money to help with their education.

▶ Trust funds are generally ineffective at sheltering money from the need analysis process, and can backfire on you.

▶ If you have a second home, and you need a home equity loan, take the equity loan on the second home and pay off the mortgage on the primary home.

ADDITIONAL RESOURCES

The following are additional resources available to someone looking to pay for their additional education/training.

Scholarship Search Services

If you find financial aid information overwhelming, or if you simply don't have the time to do the footwork yourself, you may want to hire a scholarship search service. Be aware that a reasonable price is $30 to $50. If the service wants to charge more, investigate it carefully. Scholarship search services usually only provide you with a list of six or so sources of scholarships that you then need to check out before applying.

To find a scholarship search service, use any search engine on the Web and enter the keyword or search phrase, "Scholarship Search." A rather long directory of related websites will be displayed. Be sure to shop around for the best deals in terms of finding a company or organization that will be the most helpful in finding you scholarship opportunities based on your personal situation. Scholarships.com (www.scholarships.com) is just one such online-based company that helps students pinpoint scholarship opportunities and apply for them.

If you're still in high school and you haven't yet filled out the ETS Student Search Service form or the ACT Student Profile form, check "yes" in the box asking if you wish to release your information to scholarship programs.

Books and Pamphlets

▶ *The Student Guide*. Published by the U.S. Department of Education, this is *the* handbook about federal aid programs. To order a copy, call 800-4-FED-AID.

▶ *Looking for Student Aid*. Published by the U.S. Department of Education, this is an overview of sources of information about financial aid. To order a copy, call 800-4-FED-AID.

▶ *How Can I Receive Financial Aid for College?* Published from the Parent Brochures ACCESS ERIC website. Order a copy by calling 800-LET-ERIC or write to ACCESS ERIC, Research Blvd. MS 5F, Rockville, MD 20850-3172.

▶ *Annual Register of Grant Support.* Chicago: Marquis, Annual.

▶ *A's and B's of Academic Scholarships.* Alexandria, VA: Octameron, Annual.

▶ *Chronicle Student Aid Annual.* Moravia, NY: Chronicle Guidance, Annual.

▶ *College Blue Book. Scholarships, Fellowships, Grants and Loans.* New York: Macmillan, Annual.

▶ *College Financial Aid Annual.* New York: Prentice-Hall, Annual.

▶ *Directory of Financial Aids for Minorities* and *Directory of Financial Aids for Women.* San Carlos, CA: Reference Service Press, Biennial.

▶ *Don't Miss Out: The Ambitious Student's Guide to Financial Aid.* Robert and Ann Leider. Alexandria, VA: Octameron, Annual.

▶ *Financial Aids for Higher Education.* Dubuque: Wm. C. Brown, Biennial.

▶ *Financial Aid for the Disabled and Their Families.* San Carlos, CA: Reference Service Press, Biennial.

▶ *Paying Less for College.* Princeton: Peterson's Guides, Annual.

Another method of finding books specifically about scholarships, financial aid and/or student loans is to visit an online bookseller, such as Barnes & Noble Online (www.bn.com) or Amazon.com (www.amazon.com) and enter a search phrase that's appropriate to what you're looking for.

Telephone Numbers and Addresses

▶ Federal Student Aid Information Center, P.O. Box 84, Washington, DC 20044, 319-337-5665

▶ 800-4-FED-AID (800-433-3243)

▶ 800-MIS-USED (800-647-8733) for suspicion of fraud, waste, or abuse of federal aid

▶ ACT American College Testing program, 916-361-0656, for forms submitted to the need analysis servicer

▶ College Scholarship Service (CSS), 609-771-7725; TDD 609-883-7051

▶ Need Access/Need Analysis Service, 800-282-1550

▶ Selective Service, 847-688-6888

▶ Immigration and Naturalization Services (INS), 415-705-4205

▶ Internal Revenue Service (IRS), 800-829-1040

▶ Social Security Administration, 800-772-1213

▶ National and Community Service Program (Americorps), 800-94-ACORPS

▶ FAFSA on the WEB Processing/Software Problems, 800-801-0576

Websites

As a future webmaster, the following online-based resources will be useful for helping you locate the funds needed to pay for your education/training.

▶ One of the most comprehensive websites is www.finaid.org. It has many pages addressing special situations, such as international students, bankruptcy, defaulting on student loans, divorced parents, financially unsupportive parents, and myths about financial aid.

▶ Another equally excellent website is FastWEB at www.fastweb.com. If you answer a few simple questions (such as geographical location and age), you will receive a list of scholarships for which you may qualify. Their database is updated regularly, and your list will be updated when new scholarships are added that fit your profile. FastWEB boasts that every day more than 20,000 students access the site.

▶ *The Student Guide* (www.ed.gov/prog_info/SFA/StudentGuide/2000-1/index.html) is one of the most comprehensive resources on student financial aid from the U.S. Department of Education. Grants, loans, and work-study are the three major forms of student financial aid available through the federal Student Financial Assistance Programs.

▶ CollegeNET (www.collegenet.com/about/index.html) is a portal so that students can apply to college over the Web. It includes helpful information on financial aid and student loans/scholarships. Applicants complete, file, and pay for their admissions applications directly on the site and completely on the Internet. Applicants can apply to over 500 colleges and universities who have contracted with CollegeNET.

▶ Using any Web-based search engine, enter the search phrase "financial aid" or "scholarships" to find other online resources.

▶ Software for EFC calculators and financial aid planning and advice can be found at www.finaid.org/calculators.

FINANCIAL AID ACRONYMS KEY

COA	Cost of Attendance
CWS	College Work-Study
EFC	Expected Family Contribution
EFT	Electronic Funds Transfer
ESAR	Electronic Student Aid Report
ETS	Educational Testing Service
FAA	Financial Aid Administrator
FAF	Financial Aid Form
FAFSA	Free Application for Federal Student Aid
FAO	Financial Aid Office
FDSLP	Federal Direct Student Loan Program
FFELP	Federal Family Education Loan Program
FSEOG	Federal Supplemental Educational Opportunity Grant
FWS	Federal Work-Study
GSL	Guaranteed Student Loan
PC	Parent Contribution
PLUS	Parent Loan for Undergraduate Students
SAP	Satisfactory Academic Progress
SC	Student Contribution
SLS	Supplemental Loan for Students
USED	U.S. Department of Education

Having the desire to obtain additional training so that you can pursue a career as a webmaster and in the IT field is admirable, not to mention a smart career path strategy. No matter what your personal financial situation is, chances are you'll be able to find the funds necessary to pay for the education and training you need. Make sure that you carefully explore all of your options, including financial aid, scholarships, and various types of loans. Making a significant financial investment in your future right now will no doubt pay for itself many times over once you land a high-paying job with limitless career advancement potential.

THE INSIDE TRACK

Who: Brian Murillo

What: Technology Intern

Where: LearningExpress, New York, NY

INSIDER'S STORY

I was born with an Atari 2600 in my hands. From the time I was two, all I did was play video games. I had Nintendo, Coleco, Genesis—everything. My dad and brother-in-law were into computers; everything they learned, they showed me. By the time I was 6, I was doing stuff in DOS. I learned how to read and use computers simultaneously. But what I really wanted to do was make video games, so when my brother told me that I needed to learn how to program to make video games, I got into computers.

So far, I've finished three years of college working toward computer science major. I'm a Microsoft Certified Professional and I'm working towards certification as a Microsoft Systems Engineer. In my own experience, though, I think that work experience is very important. Schools usually give you a lot of theory and mathematical concepts, but in terms of practical application, on-the-job experience is a great learning tool.

I would encourage students who are already in college and are trying to be webmasters or IT professionals to pursue jobs at their schools. One of my first jobs was as a roaming administrator for the residential computing network. My job was to make sure all the computers in all the labs were running; I would install things, fix things, tear down machines, and put them back together.

For people not intending to complete a college degree, I think the best thing to do is take a certification course. Definitely try to pursue education, though, because it does open doors for you. Companies may not want to hire you without some education.

INSIDER'S ADVICE

If someone tells you that a computer works because it's plugged in, you have to say that's not good enough for me, and dig deeper for more understanding of how things work. And, there's no limit in the amount of education you can give yourself, whether it's from a friend, at work, or through a course or book. In this field, I think curiosity—above all else—is key. You also have to stick with it, even when you get frustrated. There's always an answer, and always more to learn.

CHAPTER four

HOW TO LAND YOUR FIRST JOB

THIS CHAPTER explains how to find a job after you complete your training. First you'll learn how to conduct your job search through networking, research, reading industry publications, using classified ads, utilizing online resources, visiting job fairs, and contacting job hotlines. Knowing how to find the best job opportunities is the first part of the whole job search process. In the next chapter, you'll get tips on how to write your resume. In Chapter 6, you'll discover the secrets of participating in a successful job interview and ultimately learn how to land your first job in the webmaster and IT field.

ONCE YOU'VE completed your training program and you have a degree or certification that's in demand by employers, you'll be just about ready to kick off your job search. The good news is that there are a lot of available jobs in the IT field because it is a booming industry. Companies of all sizes are staking their ground in cyberspace, and these companies need qualified personnel to create, manage, and maintain their websites.

The bad news, however, is that the job search process can be a time consuming and stressful one. By taking an organized approach and utilizing the resources available to you—such as the Internet—the whole process can be extremely manageable.

CONDUCTING YOUR JOB SEARCH

Finding the right job always begins with research. You need to know exactly what webmaster or other IT-related jobs you're qualified to fill, what jobs are available, where the jobs can be found, and what it'll take for you to land one of those jobs.

Luckily, a lot of material is available to guide your search. By utilizing techniques ranging from answering help-wanted ads and networking, to attending job fairs and tapping the power of the Internet, you can confidently find your first job in the computer field.

If your goal is to work as a webmaster or in a related field, one of the first things you'll need to do is create an online portfolio for yourself. You'll want to create your own website that showcases your capabilities, knowledge, and skills. After all, if you're going to be designing, managing, or maintaining websites and pages for a company, chances are that employer will want to see samples of your work before you get hired.

Just as an artist or graphic designer creates a portfolio to showcase past achievements, or a musician/recording artist creates a demo of music before approaching record labels, it's an excellent strategy to develop an online presence for yourself as a future webmaster. This electronic or online resume/portfolio not only tells your story, but also demonstrates your proficiency using the skills and knowledge an employer will be looking for. It's one thing to say, "Sure, I'm an advanced Flash programmer and can create stunning animations for any website." It's another thing altogether to be able to demonstrate that skill by showing an employer actual animations you've created using Macromedia's Flash.

Of course, as you kick off your job search efforts, you'll still need a traditional resume, but for many webmaster-related jobs you'll also want to develop a portfolio of your work so you can demonstrate and prove your skills to a potential employer. Even if you don't have any real-world work experience designing professional websites, you can still create sample websites or pages that will demonstrate your proficiency using the latest programming tools, technology, and techniques.

TAKING A DEADLINE-ORIENTED APPROACH TO YOUR JOB SEARCH EFFORTS

Landing a job is often a confusing, stressful, and extremely time-consuming task. You have to find job opportunities, create a resume, write cover letters, schedule interviews, research companies, participate in interviews, make follow-up calls, and keep track of all the potential employers you meet or correspond with. You will also want to put together a portfolio of your work as a webmaster (or graphic designer, animator or Web page designer, for example). One way to help take the stress out of this whole procedure is to adopt an organized, deadline-oriented approach for finding yourself a job in the webmaster and IT field.

Begin by acquiring a personal planner, such as a Day-Timer®, or a personal digital assistant (PDA), such as the Palm III™ or Palm V™ (www.palm.com). Before actually starting your job search, make a list of everything you'll have to accomplish in order to land a job. Break up the big tasks into lots of smaller ones, which are easier to accomplish. If you have to write or update your resume, or get your resume printed, add it to your list. If you need to buy outfits to wear to interviews, that too goes on your list. Once your list is complete, write down how long you think each task will take to accomplish.

Next, prioritize your list. Determine what tasks need to be done immediately, and which items can wait until later in the job search process. Estimate approximately how long it will take to accomplish each task and create a schedule for yourself with deadlines.

Using your personal planner, calendar, or PDA, start at today's date and enter in each job search-related task, one at a time. Under your list of tasks to complete, add items like "check the help wanted ads" and "update resume." Leave yourself enough time to accomplish each task, and in your planner, mark down the date when each task should be completed by.

Keep meticulous notes in your planner or on your PDA. Write down everything you do, who you make contact with, the phone numbers and addresses of your contacts, what is discussed on the phone or during interviews, what follow-up actions need to be taken, and even what you wore to each interview. Throughout your job search process, keep your planner or PDA with you at all times. Refer to it and update it often to ensure that you remain on-track.

To demonstrate that you are a well-organized person, during the interview refer to your planner or PDA and don't be afraid to jot down notes. If a potential employer wants to schedule a second interview, take out your planner or PDA, and schedule an appointment on the spot.

PLAYING THE FIELD AND UNDERSTANDING WHAT'S OUT THERE

Many job seekers limit their potential success by limiting their job search. Keep in mind that almost every industry requires skilled computer specialists, IT professionals, and webmasters, because virtually every industry now relies heavily on computers to keep its businesses operating. Schools, hospitals, publishers, banks, retail shops, Internet service providers, website design firms, accounting firms, and law firms, for example, all use computers and all hire IT specialists. Furthermore, more and more companies are establishing themselves on the World Wide Web, which has created a demand for skilled web technicians, website designers, and other people with a strong knowledge of the Internet.

As you begin your job search, don't restrict your search to companies within the computer or Internet industry, such as Intel, America Online, Yahoo!, IBM, Compaq, or Oracle. Sure, the computer companies hire webmaster and IT professionals, but so does virtually every other company in existence. You may find your dream job lies in another field or industry altogether. Yes, it's possible to be a webmaster and work for a major department store chain, retail shop, doctor's office, law firm, or even a car dealership.

Start your job search by making a list of all the fields that interest you. Think carefully about the type of environment in which you might feel most comfortable working. Some of your options include: a large national company with a corporate environment, a small start-up company with a family feel, or something in between.

FINDING THE JOBS AVAILABLE

If you're wondering where to find the best job opportunities, the following section will help you pinpoint what jobs are available. Keep in mind, however, that the majority of really good jobs are never formally advertised. To find out about them, you'll need to tap your networking skills. In some cases, a company that has not yet expanded its reach into cyberspace may not yet have the need for a webmaster. Yet, once you approach the potential employer with a detailed plan for developing the company's website or e-commerce site, for example, you may find yourself getting hired to spearhead these efforts. You may also land a job simply by contacting a company with a relatively small online presence and offering suggestions on how the company can inexpensively expand its online operations and improve the website's efficiency, functionality, or profitability.

When it comes to finding job openings, the following sections will give you an idea of the resources available to you.

Help Wanted Classified Ads

Classified ads are an easy and inexpensive way to job hunt; the newspaper comes right to your doorstep, and it contains pages of job openings geared to computer professionals. When you use the classified ads as a resource, look in the computer section for job titles containing the words "webmaster," "Web content developer," "e-commerce specialist," "IT professional," or "Certified Internet Webmaster." You can also often search Help Wanted ads online by visiting the website of your local major daily newspaper. For example, in the Boston area, the Help Wanted ads published in *The Boston Herald* newspaper can also be accessed online at www.jobfind.com.

The problem with relying solely on the classified ads for your job search is that the same paper that comes to your doorstep also arrives at the doorsteps of several thousands of your neighbors. For every job listed, dozens of applicants will send a resume to the employer, and you will be competing with all of them. Don't ignore the ads; just know that you need to use additional job search strategies to maximize your success. Also, if the ad appears in the Sunday newspaper, respond to it first thing Monday morning. Don't wait until the middle or end of the week.

As you look for jobs, first make a list of all the different job titles you'd be qualified to fill. After all, there is little continuity between job titles in the various industries. Make sure you read the job requirements listed within the Help Wanted ad or job description before determining whether or not you're qualified to fill the webmaster or IT-related position.

Job Directories

The library and local chamber of commerce maintain directories of employers in your area. Two excellent sources organized specifically for job hunters are *The World Almanac National Job Finder's Guide* (St. Martin's Press) and the *Job Bank* series (Adams, Inc.). There are brief job descriptions and online resources in the *Job Finder's Guide*; the *Job Bank* books are published by geographic region and contain a section profiling specific companies, with contact information for major employers in your region sorted by industry. Once you've identified companies in your area of interest, use the resources at your local library to learn more about them. Your librarian can help you find public information about local firms, including the names of all the company's officers, the number of employees, a brief description of the company, and contact information. Also, be sure to tap the Internet as a research tool for finding job opportunities and learning about potential employers.

School Career Placement Centers

Many colleges, universities, and technical schools have a career guidance office that receives job openings from a variety of local employers. Many of these guidance offices also offer resume-writing assistance and interview skills training. If you have access to one, make use of it.

Online Resources

One of the fastest growing resources for job searching is the Internet. Companies of all sizes now have websites that describe their business and list job openings. In addition, the federal government, many state and local governments, and several national job banks have websites with thousands of job listings all over the country. Most libraries and many schools allow free Internet access to their patrons. In fact, the Public Library Association has published its own *Guide to Internet Job Searching*.

This book contains an entire section devoted to search techniques for the Internet that will help you find exactly what you are looking for. If you are interested in working for a particular company, use the Internet search for its website and find out if it posts job openings.

If you are looking for a government job, check out www.jobsfed.com. This site lists over 10,000 federal jobs. Also search the Internet to see if your state's placement office has a website.

Career-Related Websites

On the World Wide Web, there are literally thousands of career-related websites. Some of these sites offer how-to advice about landing a job. Others offer a database of job listings that can be searched by region, industry, job type, salary, position, job title, or almost any other criteria. There are also resume databases that allow applicants to post their resumes for recruiters to read. If you need assistance creating your resume, there are professional resume writers who you can hire directly off the Web—many of whom also have informative websites of interest to job seekers.

The Web is an extremely powerful job search tool that can not only help you find exciting job opportunities, but you can also research companies, network with other people in your field, and obtain valuable career-related advice.

Using any Internet Search Engine or portal, you can enter a keyword such as: "resume," "job," "career," "job listings," or "help wanted" to find thousands of websites of interest to you. You can also use a keyword search that describes the type of job you're looking to fill, such as "webmaster." The following is a listing of just some of the online resources available to you:

- 1st Impressions Career Site—www.1st-imp.com
- 6-Figure Jobs—www.6figurejobs.com
- ABA Resume Writing—www.abastaff.com/career/resume/resume.htm
- About.com—http://jobsearch.about.com/jobs/jobsearch/msubrespost.htm
- Accent Resume Writing—www.accent-resume-writing.com/critiques
- Advanced Career Systems—www.resumesystems.com/career/Default.htm
- America's Employers—www.americasemployers.com
- America's Job Bank—www.ajb.dni.us
- Best Jobs USA—www.bestjobsusa.com
- Career & Resume Management for the 21st Century—http://crm21.com
- Career Builder—www.careerbuilder.com
- Career Center—www.jobweb.org/catapult/guenov/res.html#explore
- Career Creations—www.careercreations.com
- Career Express—www.careerxpress.com
- Career Spectrum—www.careerspectrum.com/dir-resume.htm
- Career.com—www.career.com
- CareerMosaic—www.careermosaic.com
- CareerNet—www.careers.org
- CareerPath—www.careerpath.com
- CareerWeb—www.cweb.com
- College Central Network—http://employercentral.com
- Competitive Edge Career Service—www.acompetitiveedge.com
- Connect Me.com—http://connectme.com/advice/resume/index.html
- Creative Keystrokes—www.creativekeystrokes.com
- Creative Professional Resumes—www.resumesbycpr.com
- Curriculum Vitae Tips—www.cvtips.com
- First Job: The website—www.firstjob.com
- First Resume Store International—www.resumestore.com
- Gary Will's Worksearch—www.garywill.com/worksearch
- JobBank USA—www.jobbankusa.com

- JobLynx—www.joblynx.com
- JobSource—www.jobsource.com
- JobStar—http://jobsmart.org/tools/resume
- JobTrack—www.jobtrack.com
- Kaplan Online Career Center—www.kaplan.com
- My Job Coach—www.myjobcoach.com
- National Business Employment Weekly Online—www.nbew.com
- Occupational Outlook Handbook—stats.bls.gov/oco/oco1000.htm
- Professional Association of Resume Writers—www.parw.com/homestart.html
- Proven Resumes—www.free-resume-tips.com
- Proven Resumes—www.provenresumes.com
- Quintessential Careers—www.quintcareers.com/resres.html
- Rebecca Smith's eResumes & Resources—www.eresumes.com
- Resumania—www.resumania.com
- Resume Broadcaster—www.resumebroadcaster.com
- Resume Magic—www.liglobal.com/b_c/career/res.shtml
- Resume Plus—www.resumepls.com
- Resume.com—www.resume.com
- Resumedotcom—www.resumedotcom.com
- Salary.com—www.salary.com
- Taos Careers—www.taos.com/resumetips.html
- The Boston Herald's Job Find—www.jobfind.com
- The Confident Resume—www.tcresume.com
- The Employment Guide's Career Web—www.cweb.com/jobs/resume.html
- The Monster Board—www.monster.com
- The Resume—www.wm.edu/csrv/career/stualum/resmdir/contents.htm
- The Wall Street Journal Careers—www.careers.wsj.com
- Vault.com—www.vaultreports.com/jobBoard/SearchJobs.cfm
- Yahoo Careers—http://careers.yahoo.com

Job Placement Firms

Generally speaking, two types of businesses specialize in job placement: employment agencies and contract houses. Employment agencies search for full-time employment opportunities for you. Sometimes you are required to pay their fee; sometimes your new employer will pay it. Be sure to find out who is responsible for paying the fee before you sign up with an agency. After you are placed in a job, your relationship with the placement agency ends.

A contract house places you in short- or long-term contract positions for an ongoing fee paid by the employer (for example: the employer pays $20 per hour for your skills; you make $15 per hour, and the contract house makes $5 per hour). When your contract with a particular company is over, the contract house finds another contract position for you. You are not an employee of the companies you contract with, and you do not receive benefits from them. An advantage of contracting is that you get a variety of experiences.

Job Fairs

Attending job or career fairs is another way to find employment as an IT professional or webmaster. Job fairs bring together a number of employers under one roof, usually at a school, hotel, convention center, or civic center. These employers send representatives to the fair to inform prospective employees about their company, accept resumes, and, occasionally, to conduct interviews for open positions. Most of these job fairs also hold seminars for attendees covering such topics as resume writing, job hunting strategies, and interviewing skills.

To find the next scheduled job fair in your area, contact the information office of the convention center or civic center nearest you and ask if there's a job fair on their upcoming events calendar. If not, the local newspaper or state unemployment office may have relevant information. Or, if you're still in school, ask the career counseling center about job fairs.

While it's true that you'll most likely be competing with many other job seekers at a job fair, your opportunity to impress an employer is far greater during an in-person meeting than if you simply respond to a help wanted ad by submitting your resume. By attending a job fair, your appearance, level of preparation, what you say and how you say it, and your body language can be used to help make an employer interested in hiring you. When you go to a job fair, your goal is to get invited to the company at a later date for a formal, in-person interview. Since you'll have limited time with an employer at a job fair—typically between five and ten minutes—it's very rare that an employer will hire someone on the spot, but this does happen.

Preparation on your part is vital. Determine beforehand which employers will be there and whether or not you have the qualifications to fill the job openings available. Begin your research by visiting the website created to promote the job fair you are interested in attending. The website typically lists detailed information about the companies attending and what types of jobs participating employers are looking to fill. Once you pinpoint the employers you're interested in, do research on those companies, as if you're preparing for an actual in-person job interview.

Determine exactly how your qualifications and skills meet the needs of employers in which you are interested. In addition, you should develop a list of questions to ask the employer during your in-person meeting at the job fair. Showing a sincere interest in working for an employer and asking questions that demonstrate your interest will help set you apart from the competition in a positive way.

Bring plenty of copies of your resume to the job fair. Begin your visit to the job fair by visiting the companies you're most interested in working for as early in the day as possible. As the day goes on, the people working the job fair tend to get tired and may be less responsive—especially if they've already met with several dozen potential applicants.

You should also be prepared to answer questions about why you want to work for that company and how your skills and qualifications make you qualified to fill one of the positions the employer has available.

As you meet with people, collect business cards, and follow up your meetings later that day with a short letter, e-mail, or fax thanking the person you met with for their time. Use this correspondence to reaffirm your interest in working for an employer.

Job Hotlines

Many companies maintain a list of job openings through telephone hotlines. These hotlines are a great way to find jobs with specific companies without having to contact the human resources department directly. Using a touch-tone telephone, you can listen to a company's list of available jobs and requirements. Job hotlines usually are not found in the phone book, but *The National Job Hotline Directory*, updated every year, lists thousands of job hotlines all over the country, including those for the state and federal government. It is available at most local libraries and bookstores.

Industry Newsletters and Magazines

Knowing how to stay on top of changes in your field will help make you a more attractive candidate for any job. One of the best ways to track industry trends is by reading newspapers and publications geared toward that industry. These publications will announce breaking news and explain its significance. Being up on industry news will help convince potential employers that you will be a valuable asset to their company.

You need to watch two types of trends: those specific to the computer industry and those specific to the company/industry you want to work in. Articles in computer-related magazines, e-zines (online magazines), and journals can help you keep up with emerging trends in the direction of future computer development. This knowledge will make you more noticeable as a prospective employee and more valuable as a full-time employee. You will bring a strategic vision to your position based on your informed insight.

You also need to be aware of trends in the industry or company of your choice—medical, state universities, banks, and so on. For instance, an article in the business section of your local newspaper announcing a new vice president may signal that the company is either expanding or changing direction and might soon be hiring new employees. An article in your area's business newspaper describing the legislature's plans to impose a new law that will affect local businesses might lead you to either approach or avoid those companies in your job search. A series of articles in an industry publication about the future of business in that industry should help you focus your job-hunting strategy.

Depending on what aspect of the computer industry you choose to work in, chances are there's an industry-oriented publication that caters to your professional interests. One of the best ways to keep up on the latest news and developments in your industry is to read as many industry publications as possible. Reading back issues of these magazines will also help bring you up to speed on what's happening. For the Internet industry, publications like *InfoWorld, The Industry Standard, HotWired, USA Today: Tech, E-Business World, Internet Week*, and *InternetWorld* should be part of your regular reading list.

NETWORKING

You've heard the expression "It's not what you know, it's who you know." To be honest, it's both. What you know is vital to getting a job; who you know can also help.

What Is Networking?

Networking is simply getting to know people in your industry and maintaining contact with them. Networking relationships can provide many benefits:

- ▶ mentoring
- ▶ contacts within a prospective employment company
- ▶ information about emerging technology
- ▶ cutting-edge training
- ▶ information about trends in the industry

Making Good Contacts

How do you begin networking? You probably already have. Any time you talk to someone you meet about your mutual interests in the computer field or emerging technology, you have made a contact. Of course, the contact will be short-lived if the person walks away before you get a name and phone number. Make a habit of exchanging business cards with people you meet in your field. You can get your own business cards even before you land your first job. Include your name, phone number, and a (potential) job title, such as webmaster or Internet content developer, Web programmer, or graphic designer.

However, you don't want to exchange cards with everyone you meet. You'll run out of your own cards and places to store all the cards you collect. So who should you consider a contact? Network with people you meet through family and friends who work in the IT field—especially if they have experience you can learn from—and who are in a position to hire new webmasters and IT professionals. Don't discount your peers—consider peers who are energetic, personally motivated, and advancing in their field as good contacts too.

Expanding Your Contact List

If you take a seminar from a working professional, keep the contact alive. Or, if a computer professional speaks to one of your classes, ask the person a few questions and for his or her business card. Then follow up the next day with a phone call or e-mail, saying thank you or asking an additional question.

Also consider requesting informational interviews at companies that interest you. An informational interview is one in which you meet with someone to find out about the company—what it does, what sorts of positions are available or may be in the future. This is discussed further in the Interview section later in this chapter. An informational interview is an excellent opportunity for you in many ways:

▶ You learn more about how companies work.

▶ You gain interview experience.

▶ You gain a contact that might help you get a job in the future.

Maintaining Your Contacts

It is important to maintain contacts once you have established them. Try to contact people again within two weeks of meeting them. You can always send a thank-you note, ask a question, or send a piece of information related to your conversation with them. This contact cements your meeting in their minds; they will remember you more readily when you meet them again. If you haven't been in contact with some people for a few months, you might send them a note or e-mail about a relevant new technology or article you read. Keep your name fresh in their minds.

Organizing Your Contact List

Many software packages, such as Act! 2000 (www.act.com) can help you maintain your contact list. The alternative is to use business cards on a Rolodex or a list in your day planner. A PDA is also an excellent tool for managing contacts electronically, because the unit can be taken with you when you leave your office. Try to maintain the following pieces of information about each person:

▶ name
▶ address
▶ e-mail address
▶ phone number(s)
▶ fax number
▶ company
▶ position
▶ first meeting (where, when, what topics did you discuss?)
▶ last contact (when, why, and how)

Now that you know where to find the best jobs, and you have the training to fill one or more of the job openings you find, the next step in the job search process is to create your resume and cover letter, and then actually start applying for the jobs that are of interest. The next chapter will walk you through the resume creation process.

THE INSIDE TRACK

Who: Christie Asmussen

What: Webmaster

Where: LearningExpress

INSIDER'S STORY

The first time I used a computer was in kindergarten. I would look at the screen and wonder, "How is it doing that?" I got more serious about computers in high school, and went on to study management information systems at Central Connecticut State University. At CCSU, there was a work-study program that delayed my graduation for a semester, but was worth the extra time for the real-world experience received. I'd advise anyone to try a work-study program, get an internship, or work part-time; not only do you make great contacts this way, but it also looks good on your resume.

After I got my degree, I really wanted to go to this job fair in New York, but my school wouldn't let me go because they didn't have enough invitations. Because I had heard that this was a great networking event, I was persistent and eventually got in. While I was there I got my first job with Aetna. As a junior programmer there, I realized that I wanted to learn more about setting up computers and networks, so I got a help-desk job in order to learn more about different things. At the same time, I also studied and took exams to get additional certification before arriving at my current position.

In my current position, my job is to make sure servers are working, see that there are no errors, set up monitoring systems to prevent errors, maintain the network, and support the e-mail system. I also build servers and set up the entire network architecture for our site. From a big-picture standpoint, I try to keep the company up to date with new software and infrastructure.

The thing I like most is that I get to do different things. I enjoy taking things apart and putting them together. It's similar to programming in that it requires problem solving—only with more parts and a bigger picture involved. Also, it keeps me physically active, which I like; sitting and programming all day used to drive me crazy!

INSIDER'S ADVICE

Be persistent! If you hear about a job fair, get yourself there. Pursue internships and part-time positions through your network. Don't be shy about asking for help. You'll thank yourself later.

CHAPTER five

WRITING YOUR RESUME

ONCE YOU'VE pinpointed what job opportunities you're interested in pursuing, you'll need to use a resume, cover letter, and possibly a portfolio of your work to apply for those jobs. This chapter walks you through the process of creating a resume. Your resume, combined with your cover letter and work portfolio (if applicable), are extremely important tools for landing a job. Be sure you take whatever time is necessary to create well-thought-out documents that clearly represent who you are and what qualifications you have.

WHAT GOES INTO A RESUME?

Most potential employers want to know the same basic things about you: your name/address, education/training, computer skills, and work experience. You might also include information about your career goal/objective, the professional organizations you belong to, and your professional references. The rest of this chapter will explain how to organize and present this information.

Even if you choose to hire a professional resume writer or resume preparation service, he or she will require the majority of this information in order to do a good job creating a resume on your behalf. The same holds true if you purchase off-the-shelf resume creation software for your computer. Keep in mind, the majority of these resume writing tips and strategies apply to traditional printed resumes as well as to electronic resumes.

The first section of any resume includes information about how a potential employer can contact you. The details you'll want to provide include:

Contact Information

Full Name: _____

Permanent Street Address: _____

City, State, Zip: _____

Daytime Telephone Number: _____

Evening Telephone Number: _____

Pager/Cell Phone Number (Optional): _____

Fax Number (Optional): _____

E-Mail Address: _____

Personal Website Address/Online Portfolio URL: _____

School Address (if applicable): _____

Your Phone Number at School (if applicable): _____

As a potential webmaster or IT professional, a basic requirement is that you include an e-mail address and/or personal website address on your resume. This is something that employers will expect to see. You'll also discover that some potential employers find it easier to contact applicants via e-mail. Listing a personal website address also emphasizes your website development skills, and provides potential employers with an additional way of learning more about you.

If you don't yet have an e-mail address, consider joining one of the popular online services, such as America Online (www.aol.com). Many other companies, such as Yahoo! (www.yahoo.com), Hotmail (www.hotmail.com), and Juno (www.juno.com) offer free personal and private e-mail accounts to people who already have Internet access. These free e-mail accounts can be accessed from any computer that's connected to the Internet, which means you can send and receive messages from your personal e-mail address anytime from school, your home computer, your computer at work (although this isn't recommended), a public library, or a friend's computer. If you already have your own Internet account, chances are you have an e-mail address through your Internet Service Provider (ISP).

The following questions will help you pinpoint the specific types of information that needs to go into the various sections of your resume and cover letter. By answering these questions, you'll also get to know yourself better, so you can find the job opportunities you'll prosper in and that you'll enjoy. For more information on creating your resume, be sure to read *Great Resume* (Jason R. Rich, LearningExpress, 2000).

Job/Career Objective(s)

Write a short description of the job you're seeking. Be sure to include as much information as possible about how you can use your skills to the employer's benefit. Later, you'll condense this answer into one short sentence.

_____

_____

_____

What is the job title you're looking to fill? (i.e., webmaster)

_____

What are alternate job titles you're qualified to fill? (i.e., Graphic Designer, Web Animator, Web Content Developer, Web Programmer, e-Commerce Specialist, Certified Internet Webmaster)

_____

_____

_____

Educational Background

List the most recent college or university you've attended: _____
City/State:_____
What year did you start? _____
Graduation month/year: _____
Degree(s) and/or award(s) earned: _____
Your major:_____

Your minor(s):_____

List some of your most impressive accomplishments, extracurricular activities, club affiliations, etc.:_____

_____

List specialized computer courses you've taken that help qualify you for the job you're seeking: _____

_____

_____

Grade point average (GPA): _____

Other college/university you've attended: _____

City/State:_____

What year did you start? _____

Graduation month/year: _____

Degree(s) and/or award(s) earned: _____

Your major: _____

Your minor(s):_____

List some of your most impressive accomplishments, extracurricular activities, club affiliations, etc.:_____

List specialized computer courses you've taken that help qualify you for the job you're seeking: _____

_____

_____

Grade point average (GPA):_____

High school attended: _____

City/State: _____

Graduation date:_____

Grade point average (GPA): _____

List the names and phone numbers of one or two current or past professors/teachers (or guidance counselors) you can contact about obtaining a letter of recommendation or list as a reference:_____

_____

_____

_____

On your actual resume, you probably don't want to list your GPA or your class ranking, unless you've graduated in the very top of your class. For now, however, include the information within this questionnaire.

Personal Skills and Abilities

Your personal skill set (the combination of skills you possess) is something that differentiates you from everyone else. Skills that are marketable in the workplace aren't always taught in school, however.

Your ability to manage people; stay cool under pressure; remain organized; surf the Internet; use software applications (such as FrontPage 2000); program in HTML, Java, Flash and/or C++; speak in public; communicate well in writing; communicate in multiple languages; or perform research are all examples of marketable skills.

When reading job descriptions or help wanted ads, pay careful attention to the wording used to describe what the employer is looking for. As you customize your resume for a specific employer, you'll want to match up what the employer is looking for with your own qualifications as closely as possible. Try to utilize the wording provided by the employer within the help wanted ad or job description.

For example, an employer may list the following as job requirements for a webmaster. (The following are actual requirements taken from a help wanted ad published by a Wall Street investment bank looking to hire a webmaster):

▶ Intranet technologies (Web Server, Browser, HTML, ASP)
▶ Operating Systems (NT, Solaris 2.8)
▶ Knowledge of Scripting (Perl, Java, Lotus Script)
▶ Intra-networking including TCP/IP
▶ Web Server administration (IIS, NES)
▶ Web Application Servers (WebLogic, WebSphere)
▶ Netscape Proxy server
▶ Directory structure (LDAP)

You'll want to address that you have these specific skills in your resume and cover letter, as well as during your interview. If you're putting together a portfolio to showcase your work, you'll also want to demonstrate competency in these areas.

What do you believe is your most marketable skill? Why? _____

_____

_____

_____

List three or four specific examples of how you have used this skill in the past while at work. What was accomplished as a result? List specific software packages, programming tools and/or technology you've utilized.

1. _____

2. _____

3. _____

4. _____

What are keywords or buzzwords that can be used to describe your skills?

_____

_____

What is another of your marketable skills? _____

_____

_____

Provide at least three examples of how you've used this skill in the workplace:

1. _____

2. _____

3. _____

What unusual or unique skills do you possess that help you stand out from other applicants applying for the same types of positions as you?

_____

_____

_____

How have you already proven this skill is useful in the workplace?

_____

_____

_____

What computer skills do you possess? _____

_____

_____

What computer software packages are you proficient in (such as Microsoft Office—Word, Excel, PowerPoint, FrontPage, etc.)? _____

_____

_____

Thinking carefully, what skills do you believe you currently lack? _____

_____

What skills do you have, but that need to be polished or enhanced in order to make you a more appealing candidate?

_____

What options are available to you to either obtain or brush up on the skills you believe need improvement (for example: evening/weekend classes at a college or university, adult education classes, seminars, books, home study courses, on-the-job-training, etc.):

_____

_____

In what time frame could you realistically obtain this training? _____

_____

_____

_____

Work/Employment History

Most recent employer:_____

City, State:_____

Year you began work:_____

Year you stopped working (write "Present" if still employed):_____

Job title:_____

Job description:_____

_____

Reason for leaving:_____

What were your three proudest accomplishments while holding this job?

   1. _____

   2. _____

   3. _____

Contact person at the company who can provide a reference:_____

_____

Contact person's phone number:_____

Annual salary earned:_____

Employer: _____

City, State:_____

Year you began work:_____

Year you stopped working (write "Present" if still employed):_____

Job title:_____

Job description:_____

_____

Reason for leaving:_____

What were your three proudest accomplishments while holding this job?

   1. _____

   2. _____

   3. _____

Contact person at the company who can provide a reference:_____

Contact person's phone number:_____

Annual salary earned:_____

Complete these employment-related questions for all of your previous employers, including part-time or summer jobs held while in school, as well as temp jobs and internships.

When it actually comes time to communicate with potential employers, you probably won't want to reveal your past earning history. You will want this information available to you as reference, however, when you begin negotiating your future salary, benefits, and overall compensation package.

Military Service (If Applicable)

Branch of service you served in:_____

Years served:_____

Highest rank achieved: _____

Decorations or awards earned: _____

Special skills or training you obtained:_____

Professional Accreditations and Licenses

List any and all of the professional accreditations and/or licenses you have earned thus far in your career. Be sure to highlight items that directly relate to the job(s) you'll be applying for._____

_____

_____

_____

Hobbies and Special Interests

List any hobbies or special interests you have that are not necessarily work-related, but that potentially could separate you from the competition. Can any of the skills utilized in your hobby be adapted for the workplace?

_____

_____

_____

_____

What nonprofessional clubs or organizations do you belong to or actively participate in? _____

_____

_____

_____

_____

Personal/Professional Ambitions

What are your long-term goals?

Personal:_____

_____

Professional:_____

_____

Financial:_____

_____

For your personal, professional, and then financial goals, what are five smaller, short-term goals you can begin working toward achieving right now that will help you ultimately achieve each of your long-term goals?

Short-Term Personal Goals

1. _____
2. _____
3. _____
4. _____
5. _____

Short-Term Professional Goals

1. _____
2. _____
3. _____
4. _____
5. _____

Short-Term Financial Goals

1. _____
2. _____
3. _____
4. _____
5. _____

Will the job(s) you'll be applying for help you achieve your long-term goals and objectives? If "yes," how? If "no," why not? _____

_____

_____

_____

Describe your personal, professional, and financial situation right now:

_____

_____

_____

What would you most like to improve about your life overall? _____

_____

_____

_____

_____

What are a few things you can do, starting immediately, to bring about positive changes in your personal, professional, or financial life? _____

_____

_____

_____

_____

Where would you like to be personally, professionally, and financially five and ten years down the road? _____

_____

_____

_____

What needs to be done to achieve these long-term goals or objectives?

_____

_____

_____

_____

What are some of the qualities about yourself, your appearance, and your personality that you're most proud of? _____

_____

_____

_____

What are some of the qualities about yourself, your appearance, and your personality that you believe need improvement? _____

_____

_____

_____

What do others most like about you? _____

_____

_____

What do you think others least like about you?

_____

_____

If you decided to pursue additional education, what would you study and why? How would this help you professionally?

_____

_____

_____

If you had more free time, what would you spend it doing? _____

_____

_____

_____

List several accomplishments in your personal and professional life that you're most proud of. Why did you choose these things?

1. _____
2. _____
3. _____

4. _____

5. _____

What were your strongest and favorite subjects in school? Is there a way to incorporate these interests into the job(s) or career path you're pursuing?

_____

_____

_____

What do you believe is your biggest weakness? Why wouldn't an employer hire you?_____

_____

_____

_____

What would be the ideal atmosphere for you to work in? Do you prefer a large corporate atmosphere, working at home, or working in a small office?

_____

_____

_____

List five qualities about a new job that would make it the ideal employment opportunity for you:

1. _____

2. _____

3. _____

4. _____

5. _____

What did you like most about the last place you worked?_____

_____

_____

What did you like least about the last place you worked?_____

_____

_____

What work-related tasks are you particularly good at? _____

_____

_____

What type of coworkers would you prefer to have? _____

_____

When it comes to work-related benefits and perks, what's most important
to you? _____

_____

_____

_____

When you're recognized for doing a good job at work, how do you like to
be rewarded?_____

_____

_____

_____

If you were to write a help wanted ad describing your ideal dream job, what
would the ad say? _____

_____

_____

Using the information in the previous questionnaire, you should be able to
begin piecing together content for your resume. In terms of choosing the best
possible wording to convey your information and then formatting your
resume, follow the guidelines in this book or purchase a book that specifically
contains dozens of sample resumes which you can obtain ideas from. Whatever you do, however, never simply copy your resume right out of a book. Use
the sample resumes provided in this book and in other resume books as a
guide, but be sure the content is 100 percent accurate and customized to you.

About You

List your full name, your address, phone number, and an e-mail address (and/or Web page URL). If you live at school or if you are thinking of moving soon, include a permanent address as well as your current information.

Do not include personal information in the resume. You could endanger your chances of getting hired if you include information about your religion, marital status, race, or other personal details.

Education and Training

When listing your educational background, start with your most recent training and work backward. List your degree or certificate, the name and location of the school, and the date you graduated. Also include special programs or vendor training you have completed.

Computer Skills

Include names of software, hardware, networking protocols, programming languages, programming tools, and platforms you have worked with. Indicate your level of expertise (example: familiar with, experienced, expert).

Work Experience

List all computer-related experience, even if it isn't as a webmaster or IT professional. Also list all customer service experience you have; every job requires customer service skills. Summer employment or part-time work should be labeled as such, and you will need to specify the months in the dates of employment for positions you held for less than a year.

If you just finished your training program, you might feel like you don't have much experience to list in a resume. Not true! Think back to those grueling school projects. Getting a grade on a project was only half the project's value. You can use it now in place of experience you have not yet gained in the workplace. List special projects with their title, a description, and lessons learned.

Objective

Many resumes begin with a career goal or objective. It doesn't have to be profound or philosophical. Describe the job you want, the field in which you want to work, whether you want full- or part-time work, and whether you want employment or contract work. The purpose of the objective is to assure potential employers that they are about to read a relevant resume.

Professional Organizations

If you belong to any professional organizations list them in a separate section of your resume.

References

Employers interested in hiring you may want to speak to people who can accurately—and favorably—vouch for your ability to do the job. Make a list of everyone you feel would be a good reference—those who would highly recommend you to an employer. However, don't include your family members; this list should be made up of former supervisors, teachers, or other adults you have worked for or dealt with in the past and who know you well. Make sure you get permission from your references before listing them.

You can include references with each resume you send out, or you can simply state at the bottom of the resume that your references are available upon request. If you are responding to an advertisement, read it carefully to see if you are supposed to send references. If the ad does not mention them, you probably don't need to send them with your resume. List your references on a sheet of paper separate from your resume, but remember to include your name, address, and phone number on your reference list too.

HOW TO ORGANIZE YOUR RESUME

What your resume says is important, but how it's formatted and what it looks like on the printed page are also critical. You can organize your resume in several ways. The most common formats:

▶ chronological format
▶ skills format (also known as a functional resume)
▶ combination of chronological and skills format
▶ electronically scannable format

The Chronological Resume

The most common resume format is chronological—you summarize your work experience year by year, beginning with your current or most recent employment experience and working backward. For each job, list the dates you were employed, the name and location of the company for which you worked, and the position(s) you held.

The Skills Resume

The skills resume—also known as the functional resume—emphasizes what you can do rather than what you have done. It is useful if you have large gaps in your work history or have relevant skills that would not be properly highlighted in a chronological listing of jobs. The skills resume concentrates on your skills and qualifications. Specific jobs you've held are listed, but they are not the primary focus of this type of resume.

The Combination Resume

You may decide a combination of the chronological and skills resume would be best to highlight your skills. A combination resume allows for a mixture of your skills with a chronological list of jobs you've held. You get the best of both resumes. This is an excellent choice for students who have limited work experience and who want to highlight specific skills.

The Electronically Scannable Resume

At many large companies, all resumes from job applicants are scanned by a computer software program with optical character recognition (OCR) systems and entered into a database. Also, if you apply for jobs over the Internet via an e-mail attachment, your resume requires special formatting so it can be read electronically.

Having access to the Internet offers job seekers a wide range of resources. One of the biggest trends right now in corporate recruiting is for employers to accept resumes online via e-mail, through one of the career-related websites, or via the applicant's own website. If you're going to be applying for jobs online or submitting your resume via e-mail, you'll need to create an electronic resume (in addition to a traditional printed resume).

An electronic resume can be created and distributed in a variety of ways. Keep in mind, there are no standard guidelines to follow when creating an electronic resume, since employers use different computer systems and software. Thus, it's important you adhere to the individual requirements of each employer in terms of formatting, saving, and sending your resume electronically.

Many companies accept electronic resumes created using Microsoft Word. If you'll be creating your electronic resume using one of these software packages, pay careful attention to what format the finished document needs to be saved in before sending it to an employer. The majority of employers prefer to receive resumes in ASCII or Rich Text Format (RTF); however, some may accept .doc files (documents saved in Word format).

An alternative to creating an electronic resume using a word processor or resume creation software is to complete an online-based resume form while visiting an employer's website or a career-related site. In order to keep incoming resumes consistent in terms of formatting, many websites designed for recruiting insist that all electronic resumes be created using a predefined template. Online jobseekers can complete a detailed form that requests all pertinent resume information. The user is prompted for each piece of information separately in predefined fields. The website then formats the information automatically to meet the employer's requirements.

When completing an online-based resume form, be sure you fill in all fields with the appropriate information only. Be mindful of limitations for each field. For example, a field that allows for a job description to be entered may have space for a maximum of only 50 words, so the description you enter needs to provide all of the relevant information (using keywords), but also be written concisely. Since an electronic resume is as important as a traditional one, consider printing out the online form first and then spending time thinking about how you'll fill in each field.

Don't attempt to be clever and add information that wasn't requested in a specific field in order to provide more information about yourself to an employer. If you're only given space to enter one phone number, but you want to provide a home and cell phone number, don't use the fields for your address to enter the second phone number.

In most situations, if an employer accepts electronic resumes, chances are those resumes are imported directly into applicant tracking software. The software used by the employer extracts specific information it's programmed to seek out in the resume document you submit. If you don't provide the resume file in the appropriate format, there's a strong chance your resume will be ignored or not processed correctly.

The majority of online resume templates you'll come across on the various career-related websites and sites hosted by individual employers follow the same basic format as a traditional chronological resume; however, you'll be prompted to enter each piece of information in separate fields, and you'll most likely be limited to the number of fields you can fill in.

Some employers give applicants the option to complete an online resume form/template or send an electronic resume via e-mail. Unless your work history and other information fits nicely into the format the online form/template follows, opt to send your own electronic resume via e-mail. This will allow you to more easily customize the format you use so you can best highlight your skills and abilities.

For an electronic resume to do its job correctly, it needs to be loaded with keywords that will result in your resume getting selected when processed by a potential employer using applicant-tracking software.

When e-mailing your electronic resume directly to an employer, as a general rule, the document should be saved in an ASCII, Rich Text, or plain text file and inserted into your e-mail message or attached to an e-mail message. Contact the employer directly to see which method is preferred. The benefit to using an attached file is that all of the formatting you added to your electronic resume when you created it on your word processor (line spacing, tabs, bullets, bold text, etc.) will remain intact. If the file is sent in the body of an e-mail message, all formatting may be lost, so only the text will be received.

Due to the threat of computer viruses, however, many employers refuse to accept e-mail messages with file attachments. Thus, if you send your resume file attached to a standard e-mail message, the chances of that message simply getting deleted is very high.

When sending a resume via e-mail, the message should contain the same information as a cover letter. You can then either attach the resume file to the e-mail or paste the resume text within the message. Be sure to include your e-mail address as well as your regular mailing address and phone number(s) within all correspondence. Never assume an employer will receive your message and simply hit "reply" using their e-mail software to contact you.

No matter how you're submitting your electronic resume, be sure to proofread it carefully before hitting the "send" button. Just as with a traditional resume, spelling mistakes, grammatical errors, or providing false information won't be tolerated by employers.

When creating an electronic resume to be saved and submitted in an ASCII format, follow these formatting guidelines:

▶ Set the document's left and right margins to 6.5 inches of text displayed per line. This will ensure that the text won't automatically wrap to the next line (unless you want it to).
▶ Use a basic, 12-point text font, such as Courier or Times Roman.
▶ Avoid using bullets or other symbols. Instead of a bullet, use an asterisk (*) or a dash (-). Instead of using the percentage sign (%) for example, spell out the word "percent". (In your resume, write "15 percent," not "15%").
▶ Use the spellcheck feature of the software used to create your electronic resume and then proofread the document carefully. Just as applicant

tracking software is designed to pick out keywords from your resume that showcase you as a qualified applicant, these same software packages used by employers can also instantly count the number of typos and spelling errors in your document and report that to an employer as well.

▶ Avoid using multiple columns, tables, or charts within your document.

▶ Within the text, avoid abbreviations—spell everything out. For example, use the word "Director," not "Dir." or "Vice President" as opposed to "VP." In terms of degrees, however, it's acceptable to use terms like MBA, BA, PhD.

Knowing how to properly create and submit an electronic resume demonstrates at least some level of computer skill. If you have a personal website you want potential employers to visit in hopes they'll learn more about you, be sure the site doesn't contain personal information you don't want the employer to discover or that the employer will have no interest in such as pictures from your last vacation or photos of your pet cat. Posting your resume and support materials on a personal website can be worthwhile, especially if you're using the site as a showcase of your work or as an online portfolio. It could very well be this website that a potential employer uses to evaluate your webmaster, Web page design, or IT skills.

Properly formatting your electronic resume is important; however, what you say within your resume is what could ultimately get you hired. According to Rebecca Smith's eResumes & Resources website (www.eresumes.com), "Keywords are the basis of the electronic search and retrieval process. They provide the context from which to search for a resume in a database, whether the database is a proprietary one that serves a specific purpose, or whether it is a Web-based search engine that serves the general public. Keywords are a tool to quickly browse without having to access the complete text. Keywords are used to identify and retrieve a resume for the user.

Employers and recruiters generally search resume databases using keywords: nouns and phrases that highlight technical and professional areas of expertise, industry-related jargon, projects, achievements, special task forces, and other distinctive features about a prospect's work history."

The emphasis is not on trying to second-guess every possible keyword a recruiter may use to find your resume. Your focus is on selecting and organizing your resume's content in order to highlight those keywords for a variety of online situations. The idea is to identify all possible keywords that are appropriate to your skills and accomplishments that support the kinds of jobs you are looking for. But to do that, you must apply traditional resume writing principles to the concept of extracting those keywords from your resume. Once you have written your resume, then you can identify your strategic keywords based on how you imagine people will search for your resume.

The keywords you incorporate should support or be relevant to your job objective. Some of the best places within your resume to incorporate keywords are when listing:

► job titles
► responsibilities
► accomplishments
► skills

Industry-related buzzwords, job-related technical jargon, licenses, and degrees are among the other opportunities you'll have to come up with keywords to add to your electronic resume.

Keywords are the backbone of any good electronic resume. If you don't incorporate keywords, your resume won't be properly processed by the employer's computer system. Choosing the right keywords to include in your resume is a skill that takes some creativity and plenty of thought.

For example, each job title, job description, skill, degree, license, or other piece of information you list within your resume should be descriptive, self-explanatory, and be among the keywords the potential employer's applicant tracking software looks for as it evaluates your resume.

One excellent resource that can help you select the best keywords to use within your electronic resume is the *Occupational Outlook Handbook* (published by the U.S. Department of Labor). This publication is available, free of charge, online (http://stats.bls.gov/oco/oco1000.htm); however, a printed edition can also be found at most public libraries.

RESUME CREATION TIPS

No matter what type of resume you're putting together, here are some useful tips and strategies that will help ensure your finished document has the most impact possible when a potential employer reads it.

- ▶ Always use standard letter-sized ivory, cream, or neutral-color paper. A bright pink resume will stand out; it will also get laughed at and possibly thrown out.
- ▶ Include your name, address, and phone number on every page.
- ▶ Make sure your name is larger than anything else on the page (example: your name in a 14-point font, the rest in 12 point).
- ▶ Use a font that is easy to read, such as 12-point Times New Roman.
- ▶ Do not use more than three fonts in your resume. You want it to look like a resume, not a ransom note.
- ▶ Edit, edit, edit. Read it forward and backward. Have friends with good proofreading skills read it. Even if you have a grammar and spellchecker on your computer, you still need to review it. For instance, a spellchecker would not catch any of the errors in the following sentence: *Their are two many weighs too make errors that a computer does nut recognize.*
- ▶ Use bullet points for items in a list. If someone is glancing at your resume, it helps highlight the main points.
- ▶ Use keywords in your industry.
- ▶ Avoid using excessive graphics such as boxes, distracting lines, and complex designs.
- ▶ Be consistent when using bold, capitalization, underlining, and italics. If one company name is underlined, make sure all are underlined. Check titles, dates, and so on.
- ▶ Don't list your nationality, race, religion, or gender. Keep your resume as neutral as possible. Your resume is a summary of your skills and abilities.
- ▶ Don't put anything personal on your resume such as your birth date, marital status, height, or hobbies.
- ▶ One page is best, but do not crowd your resume. Shorten the margins if you need more space; if it's necessary to create a two-page resume,

make sure you balance the information on each page. Don't put just one section on the second page. Be careful about where the page break occurs.

▶ Keep your resume updated. Don't write "9/97 to present" if you ended your job two months ago. Do not cross out or handwrite changes on your resume.

▶ Understand and remember everything written on your resume. Be able to back up all statements with specific examples.

CREATING THE CONTENT OF YOUR RESUME

When it comes to landing a job, your resume is one of your most important sales and promotional tools. Using just one side of an 8.5″ x 11″ sheet of paper, you must convince a potential employer that you're the perfect candidate for the job opening that's available. Your resume has to be powerful, positive, attention getting, yet truthful. It should shout out to the employer, "Hire me!" not "File me!"

These 10 tips will help you create a resume that contains the information employers are looking for.

1. Start by writing out answers to the following questions to help you determine what information to include in your resume:

   ▶ What are your skills and qualifications?
   ▶ What work experience do you have that directly relates to the job you're applying for?
   ▶ Are you worth the salary you're asking for or that the job pays?
   ▶ What can you offer to the employer?
   ▶ Specifically, how will hiring you benefit the employer?
   ▶ Can you help solve problems or challenges that the employer is facing?
   ▶ What sets you apart from other people applying for the same job?

2. The main sections of a resume are: Heading, Job Objectives, Education, Accreditation and Licenses, Skills, and Experience. You may

also want to include Professional Affiliations, Military Service, and References.

3. In the Heading, include all your contact information: your full name, address, telephone number(s), fax number, pager number, and e-mail address. Also, make sure that there's an answering machine connected to the telephone number that's listed on your resume, so a potential employer can reach you anytime. Missing a message could result in a missed job opportunity.

4. The first piece of information listed in the Education section of your resume should describe the highest degree you've earned or that you're in the process of earning. When listing your education, don't include your grades, class rank, or overall average unless this information is extremely impressive and will help to set you apart from other applicants.

5. To decide what work experience to include on your resume, start by listing all of your internships, after-school jobs, summer jobs, part-time jobs, full-time jobs, and your volunteer and charitable work. Provide specific dates of employment, job titles, responsibilities, and accomplishments for each position.

6. As you sit down to write your resume, use action words—verbs that make your accomplishments sound even better. What your resume says about you, and more importantly, how it's said, is what will make your resume a powerful job search tool.

7. Choose the format that best organizes your information for an employer. Using a chronological format, your employment experience is listed in reverse chronological order, with your most recent job listed first. The functional format organizes your past work experience into categories based on actual job responsibilities. This format makes it easier to put a positive spin on large gaps in your employment history. The combination resume format is designed to answer the question, "Why are you perfect for a specific job?"

8. Make sure all of the information in your resume is well organized and is stated as succinctly as possible.

9. Print your resume on good quality, white, off-white, or cream-colored paper. Your finished resume should look neat and well balanced on the page. It should not look cluttered.

10. Before distributing your resume to potential employers, have at least two other people proofread it carefully. Even the smallest spelling or grammatical error could result in your missing out on a job opportunity.

Spending extra time on your resume is an excellent investment in your future. Pay careful attention to detail, and make sure that your resume promotes you in the best possible way. To assist in formatting and designing your resume, consider using specialized resume creation software, like Resume Maker Deluxe Edition (www.individualsoftware.com) for PC-based computers. Since the design and formatting of a resume is so important, check out one of the many books available that explain and demonstrate the resume creation process.

Successful job seekers spend many hours creating multiple drafts of their resume, fine-tuning each sentence to make sure every word makes a positive impact. A resume is a one-page composition designed to sell your skills, work experience, and educational background to a potential employer. Taking short-cuts when creating this extremely important document can have disastrous results.

To ensure your resume will be seriously considered by a potential employer, avoid making these common errors:

▶ Stretching the truth. A growing number of employers are verifying all resume information. If you're caught lying, you won't be offered a job, or you could be fired later if it's discovered that you weren't truthful.

▶ Including any references to money. This includes past salary or how much you're looking to earn within your resume and cover letter.

▶ Including on your resume the reasons why you stopped working for an employer, switched jobs, or are currently looking for a new job. Also, do not include a line in your resume saying, "unemployed" or "out of work" along with the corresponding dates in order to fill a time gap.

▶ Having a typo or grammatical error in a resume. If you refuse to take the time necessary to proofread your resume, why should an employer assume you'd take the time needed to do your job properly if you're hired?

► Using long paragraphs to describe past work experience. Consider using a bulleted list instead. Most employers will spend less than one minute initially reading a resume.

If you know the resume you're sending to an employer will be scanned into an automated applicant tracking system and not initially be read by a human, it should be created as a keyword resume. Instead of using action verbs, use nouns or adjectives to describe your skills, job responsibilities, and qualifications. For example, instead of using the action word "managed," use the word "manager" or "management." Also, be sure to use the keywords listed by the employer within the job description or help wanted ad you're responding to.

Before submitting your resume to a potential employer, read the job description carefully to ensure you have the skills, experience, and educational background the employer is looking for. In addition, if you have specific and highly marketable skills, be sure they're clearly listed. As you write, edit, and proofread your resume, make an effort to keep all of the information to the point and relevant. Remember, any less important information can be discussed during a job interview. The purpose of your resume is to get an employer interested enough so that you get invited in for an interview.

Creating a powerful resume will take time and effort. Don't be afraid to write and then rewrite your resume multiple times until you're confident it has the impact needed to set you apart from the competition.

Resume Format Sample 1

Chris McCarthy

1234 First Street
Roseville, MT 81222
406-555-5555
ChrisM@internetaddress.com

OBJECTIVE	To obtain a full-time position as a Web developer.
EDUCATION	AA degree in Computer Technology, 1998 Montana State College Missoula, MT 81224 Certificate in Netware Software, 1997 Novell Missoula, MT 81224
WORK EXPERIENCE	*Position*—Retail Associate, 1992–1995 Lighting Experts, Inc. 420 Elm Street, Suite 4A Missoula, MT 81224 *Description*—customer service and sales associate, worked extensively with computer system for sales and inventory tracking. *Position*—Retail Associate, 1995–1997 ABC Company 66 Main Street Billings, MT 81321 *Description*—supervised junior sales associates and customer service, managed inventory through computer system, and acted as store troubleshooter for computer system.
COMPUTER EXPERIENCE	Hardware—PC, Mac, Unix Software—MS Office, Lotus Notes, Adobe Acrobat, Photoshop References available upon request.

Resume Format Sample 2

[Hint: this resume was created using tables in Microsoft Word.]

Mary Page

Current Address

987 Oak Street

Oakville, ND 53902

406-555-5555

E-mail: MaryPage@InternetAddress.com

Permanent Address

1234 First Street

Watertown, ND 50298

701-555-5555

Web Page: www.marypage.com

OBJECTIVE   To obtain a full-time position as a webmaster

EDUCATION   AA degree in Computer Science, 1998

Watertown College

Watertown, ND 50298

Certificate in 123 Software, 1997

123 Incorporated

Billings, MT 81321

EXPERIENCE   Position—Help Desk, 1992–1995

J.R. Talent Agency

111 Third Avenue

Watertown, ND 50298

Description—worked extensively with computer system for sales and inventory tracking. Assisted other employees with PC-related problems.

References available upon request.

Resume Content Samples

Here are some real resumes of people looking for webmaster positions. The resumes were taken from job sites on the Internet, so we have changed the names of the candidates and businesses to protect their privacy.

Resume Content Sample 1

Andrea Bloom

5110 Apple Road
Orchardtown, PA 18298
Abloom@InternetAddress.com
(717) 555-5555

EDUCATION	1998
	Roseville College
	Roseville, PA 15762
	M.S. Applied Technology
	1996
	St. Paul's University
	Boston, MA 02142
	B.A. Psychology
	Completed senior seminar using the Internet/WWW/e-mail.
	1980
	Massachusetts Institute of Technology
	Cambridge, MA 02371
	AA—Electronics Engineering Technologist
EXPERIENCE	1/98–present
	Network Specialist—EduPublish, Boston
	Assist in management of a homogenous Novell 3.12/NT 3.51/4.0 LAN/WAN.
	Assist Help Desk personnel w/end user support of Office 2000, Notes 4.11, and remote access.

1994–1996
User Support—City Library, Boston
Assisted Network Administrators in supporting Office 2000 and Notes 4.5 on up to 200 Win95/NT/2000/OS2 workstations in a 15K nodes NT network.

1997–1998
Webmaster—State College
Configured a Windows NT 4.0 Webserver and rolled out a large website, using both Internet Information Server v.3 and Front-Page 2000.
Upgraded H/W and S/W on Web server and desktop workstations

TECHNICAL SKILLS

- Microsoft Certified Systems Engineer
- Experience maintaining, upgrading, and troubleshooting NT servers/Win2000
- Trained and experienced with a number of software applications on both stand-alone and networked desktop computers under DOS, Windows 3.x/95/2000/Me/NT 3.51/4.0
- Mac OS, including WordPerfect and Lotus123, Notes, Adobe Photoshop, Pagemaker, FileMaker Pro, Director, and MS Office Professional, Publisher, and Project. HTML experience
- Completed significant graduate coursework (3.9 GPA) in Applied Technology, including Theories of Organizations, Video Communications (using Media100), Multimedia Authoring (Director), Instructional Design, and Networking Organizations.

SKILLS

Well-versed in modern business practices. Skilled in designing, training, and providing continuing technical support for up to 300 individuals. Experience supervising the daily activities of 30–40 field engineers. Managed small to mid-sized projects effectively. Military experience as a noncommissioned officer, training and supervising enlistees. Fluent Spanish speaker.

Resume Content Sample 2

Miranda Parkinson

76 Rusty Road

Dopple, NJ 43778

615- 555-5555

Randy@internetaddress.com

EDUCATION	Rutgers University, College of Engineering
	New Brunswick, NJ 01716
	BS in Computer Engineering, May 1995
EXPERIENCE	Interstage Development, Secaucus, NJ 01821
	Engineering Intern, May 1998–July 1998

- Designed and developed security and fire alarm systems
- Webmaster (www.intertechassociates.com), Java, and CGI
- Technical writing

Lee Enterprises, Jersey City, NJ 01321

Summer Intern, June 1997–August 1997

- Updated and checked file transfers for errors between Auto-Cad and Cable-Cad systems
- Reviewed internal billing

TECHNICAL SKILLS

Auto-Cad/Cable-Cad

C/C++

Adobe Photoshop

Adobe Premiere

Macromedia Director

Microsoft Word

Microsoft Excel

Multimedia

Resume Content Sample 3

Scott White

43 Spring Street

Bemidji, ND 54983

399-555-5555

Swhite@internetadress.com

OBJECTIVE

To secure a challenging position as a programmer/analyst, webmaster, or system administrator where my skills and experience will be a valuable contribution.

EXPERIENCE

January 1998–Present

NLB Communications

Philadelphia, PA 19762

Systems Analyst/System Administrator

- Setup, maintain, automate, and document telephone applications processors and controllers.
- Utilize Perl to develop Web-based CGI application to provide interactive information services to end-user clients.
- Utilize Perl to design, code, implement, and document Web-based trouble reporting and tracking system to automate help-desk.
- Setup, maintain, and administer WindowsNT/IIS Web server.
- Perform project management duties: plan and track progress of services designed for major end-user sites.
- Interface with third parties in order to bring projects to completion.
- Provide language-level support for programmers working with Perl.

March 1997–January 1998

NLB Communications

Philadelphia, PA 19762

Programmer/Analyst

- Set up and maintained CERN HTTP Web server residing on UNIX box (Linux 2.0.23).
- Developed Web-based front-end CGI applications, using Perl to maintain and monitor systems-automation processes on the back-end.
- Set up and maintained miniSQL relational database server, utilized for Web-based CGI applications written in Perl.

- Used Perl to develop systems to automate user processes: generating billing reports and initiating the transfer of billing feeds.
- Created a Web-based solution, written in Perl and mSQL relational database, to automate monitoring of back-end processing.
- Developed Web-based work request project management system, written in Perl.
- Planned and instructed a two-day class on introductory UNIX usage.

July 1995–March 1997

NLB Communications

Philadelphia, PA 19762

Systems Analyst

- Utilized Perl to develop back-end systems to automate manual data transferring, e-mailing, and paging processes.
- Monitored and maintained FTP accounts containing customer data.
- Installed, set up, and maintained UNIX server (Linux 2.0.23) to act as an intermediary transport server transferring data via FTP across a firewall.
- Used Perl to develop the back-end systems running on the intermediary server to automate manual data transport via FTP, e-mail, and pager.

SUMMARY OF SKILLS

Over 10 years' experience working with personal computers. Three years working with client/server technology in a professional environment. Two years Perl programming utilizing CGI/Web technologies. Two years' experience with UNIX shell scripting, SQL, and relational databases including work with ODBC. Four years' experience with the Internet. Two years' experience as a part-time UNIX and Windows NT administrator. Experienced with Java, JavaScript, and VBScript including ASP. Experience with TCP/IP, HTML 3.0, Apache HTTP Server, Microsoft IIS HTTP Server, CERN HTTP Server, DOS, Windows 95, Windows NT, and MacOS 7.x/8.x.

In the next chapter, you'll learn how to complete your job search by creating cover letters to complement your resume. You'll also discover the importance of writing thank-you notes and preparing for that all-important job interview.

THE INSIDE TRACK

Who: Grant Nodine

What: Director of Web Operations

Where: NHL.com

INSIDER'S STORY

My initial exposure to computers was playing text-based games, back when Bill Gates said 640k of memory was enough for anyone. In college I was introduced to desktop publishing. It provided the ability to use computers to create things you previously could only see in magazines, and I found that to be very exciting. Desktop publishing was the killer app for me before the rise of the Internet. It allowed me to be creative in ways I hadn't thought about, like doing page layout.

Another thing that steered me toward this field was my interest in television and video production. In college, you could see the growing role of computers in that world. There was a huge opportunity for computer-savvy people to take on large amounts of responsibility very quickly. It was a pragmatic career move, because there was a high demand and I could make a good living.

I majored in media studies and political science. Back then, computer science programs were focused on turning out people with very specialized sets of skills—mostly pure programmers. Having an interdisciplinary mix of skills has served me well.

My first job was a two-and-a-half year stint at a visual effects/post production house. I mainly coordinated the production of computer graphics for TV commercials. The director of technology turned me into his system librarian, which had me rotating log files and making sure the animators didn't use up all their disk space, among other things. As time went on, my responsibilities grew. I credit that experience for giving me the skills I needed to succeed in the Internet economy.

Eventually they shut down the graphics operation due to money problems. One of the animators recruited me for a new web company which lasted about nine months before things fell apart there. But we had good clients, so four or five of my co-workers and I approached them and offered to provide the same service. We agreed on a one-year deal in which they gave us computers and two lump-sum payments. That started our company, which we named Mercury Seven.

There were seven of us in a loft with cables all over the floor. It was a loud atmosphere, because there were usually five people on the phone at the same time. Six months down the line, we had a dozen clients and 22 employees. We moved to a bigger space, and grew by leaps and bounds with even more clients.

I managed the entire technical infrastructure, which required me to wear many hats. I did everything from writing code to fixing servers to addressing the problem when somebody yelled, "I can't print!" It was hard on the budget to hire technical people who we couldn't bill to clients, and since I owned part of the company I took on a lot of that responsibility.

At some point, the growing size of the company dictated that we needed to get some venture capital or a buyer. That was the Internet heyday, and after weighing offers we accepted one from Xceed. Our stock was converted to Xceed stock, which was then traded on the NASDAQ small cap. Pretty soon, Xceed got moved to the NASDAQ main board, and we all did pretty well.

Not too long after that I got a call from a recruiter about a job at the NHL. I'm a big hockey fan, so I decided to talk to them, and I started here in June of 1999. I have a wide range of responsibilities, with the big-picture role being to make sure all pieces of the architecture are working properly. I also work with the editorial and marketing groups to implement their programs in a technical way. To break things down by percentages, I'd say that it's 30 percent troubleshooting, 20 percent coding, 30 percent staff management, and 20 percent long-term strategy.

INSIDER'S ADVICE

My advice to people wanting to get into this business is this: Don't develop technical skills to the detriment of other social skills. You need business skills, diplomatic skills, and communications skills. Unfortunately, sometimes pure technology training puts those other things off to the side.

CHAPTER six

COVER LETTERS AND THE JOB INTERVIEW PROCESS

NOW THAT you have pinpointed what type(s) of Internet-related job you plan to apply for, and you have a resume that clearly showcases your skills, work history, educational background, and qualifications, you're almost ready to begin applying for jobs in the IT field. In this chapter, you'll discover how to complement your resume with a well-written cover letter, and then discover some of the secrets of participating in a successful job interview.

COVER LETTERS

The purpose of a cover letter is to provide the reader—your potential employer—with the following information at a glance:

▶ which job you are applying for
▶ where you heard about the opening
▶ an overview of your qualifications

Keep the cover letter short. The average hiring manager reads a cover letter for approximately three seconds, so you need to get the main point across in that time.

A hiring manager may have several similar job openings at one time, so you should clearly describe the job for which you are applying. Many human resources departments track the success of their ads, so name the source (the newspaper or website, for example) in which you saw the position advertised.

The cover letter is your opportunity to summarize your qualifications effectively. While it may be impressive to list all the details of all the jobs you have held, it's better to limit your cover letter to powerful statements, such as "I have three years' experience designing websites and implementing e-commerce and secure shopping cart applications for websites operated by small retail businesses."

Address your cover letter to someone in particular, if possible. Take the time to do some investigating. Call the human resources department and ask for the name of the hiring manager or human resources representative. If it is company policy not to give out names, at least get a formal title and use that in place of the name. Try to avoid simply using *Human Resources Representative* as a name.

PARTICIPATING IN SUCCESSFUL INTERVIEWS

While there are many computer-related jobs out there, the trick to landing one of them is to sell yourself to a potential employer. While your resume will hopefully capture the attention of a human resources person, participating in an in-person job interview will provide you with the ultimate opportunity to sell yourself as the ideal job candidate.

The only way to ace an interview is by being prepared. Showing that you understand the company's needs and can fulfill them will help you convince the interviewer that you are the right person for the job. Remember the guidelines listed as you prepare for upcoming interviews.

Be Prepared

Research the company before your interview and be ready to demonstrate your knowledge. Learn what the company does and try to read recent news releases to find out where it is planning to go in the future. You can research the company in many ways: look at its Internet website, read about it in industry magazines and newspapers, and talk to people who are familiar with it. At a minimum, you should know the size of the company, what it does, and its main products or services.

Act Professionally

Take the interviewing process very seriously. You are entering the professional world, and you want to show that you will fit into that environment. It is important to be on time for your interview. Allow extra time for traffic and getting lost if the interview is in an unfamiliar location. Schedule your travel time so that you are in the lobby ten minutes before your interview starts. This will give you time to relax.

Although your interview is not a fashion show, take the time to dress properly. Depending on the culture of the company, proper attire could be anything from a suit to khakis. Make sure that your clothes are free of stains and wrinkles. And if you must make a choice, it is better to be overdressed than underdressed.

Speak Confidently

Greet your interviewer with a firm handshake and an enthusiastic smile. Speak with confidence throughout your interview and address your comments as if you assume you will be getting the job. For example, phrase your questions this way: "What would my typical day consist of?" "How many people would be on my team, and what are their areas of expertise?" Answer questions in complete sentences, not just "yes" or "no." However, don't ramble on too long answering any one question; limit your answers to under two minutes each. Many hiring managers will ask questions that don't have a right or wrong answer; they ask such questions to evaluate your problem-solving skills.

Ask Questions

You usually will be given the opportunity to ask the interviewer questions, so be prepared. Have a list ready in advance. There's much you need to know about the company and the hiring manager to determine if the company is a good fit for you. It's not just a one-way street—while you are being evaluated, you are also evaluating the company to see if it's a working environment you want. If you don't ask any questions, the hiring manager may think that you aren't interested in the position. Here are some examples of the types of questions you might want to ask in an interview:

▶ What would my typical day consist of?
▶ What would my level of responsibility be?
▶ What are the work hours?
▶ What is your management style? (Directed to the interviewer)
▶ What is the possibility for promotion in the next two years?
▶ What Web development tools does the company use?
▶ How does the company plan to expand its Internet presence in the near future?
▶ What personnel and other resources has the company already dedicated to its online presence?

Know the Interview Format

If you are interviewing with a small company, you will likely meet your interviewer right away. At a larger company, you might be asked to fill out an application in the human resources department first. You will have a copy of your resume handy, so you should be able to complete the application quickly and easily.

It is also common to meet with more than one person, especially at larger companies. You might meet with a human resources professional, and then speak with a supervisor. The interview with the person who will supervise you if you get the job will probably last longer than the other interviews. There are no hard and fast rules, because interviewing methods vary widely from company to company.

Anticipating Interview Questions You Will Be Asked

As part of your job interview preparation, determine the types of questions the interviewer will ask. Obviously, since you're applying for an IT-related job that will require specific technical skills and knowledge, the employer is going to ask you detailed questions about what skills you possess and what experience you have using those skills.

Spend time developing well thought out, complete, and intelligent answers to these anticipated questions. Thinking about answers, or even writing out answers on paper will be helpful, but what will benefit you the most is actual practice answering interview questions out loud, and having someone you trust evaluate your responses honestly.

Most of the questions you'll be asked will be pretty obvious, but be prepared for an interviewer to ask you a few questions that are unexpected. By doing this, the interviewer wants to see how you react and how well you think on your feet.

As you answer all of the interviewer's questions:

▶ Use complete sentences and proper English.
▶ Don't be evasive, especially if you're asked about negative aspects of your employment history.
▶ Never imply that a question is "stupid."
▶ Don't lie or stretch the truth.
▶ Be prepared to answer the same questions multiple times. Make sure your answers are consistent, and never reply, "You already asked me that."
▶ Never apologize for negative information regarding your past.
▶ Avoid talking down to an interviewer, or making them feel less intelligent than you are.

The following are common interview questions and suggestions on how you can best answer them:

▶ *What can you tell me about yourself?* Stress your skills and accomplishments. Avoid talking about your family, hobbies, or topics not relevant to your ability to do the job.

▶ *Why have you chosen to pursue your current career path?* Give specific reasons and examples.

▶ *In your personal or professional life, what has been your greatest failure? What did you learn from that experience?* Be open and honest. Everyone has had some type of failure. Focus on what you learned from the experience and how it helped you to grow as a person.

▶ *Why did you leave your previous job?* Try to put a positive spin on your answer, especially if you were fired for negative reasons. Company downsizing, a company going out of business, or some other reason that was out of your control is a perfectly acceptable answer. Remember, your answer will probably be verified.

▶ *What would you consider to be your biggest accomplishments at your last job?* Talk about what made you a productive employee and valuable asset to your previous employer. Stress that teamwork was involved in achieving your success, and that you work well with others.

▶ *In college, I see you were a (insert subject) major. Why did you choose (insert subject) as your major?* Explain your interest in the subject matter, where that interest comes from, and how it relates to your current career-related goals.

▶ *What are your long-term goals?* Talk about how you have been following a career path, and where you think this preplanned career path will take you in the future. Describe how you believe the job you're applying for is a logical step forward.

▶ *Why do you think you're the most qualified person to fill this job?* Focus on the positive things that set you apart from the competition. What's unique about you, your skill set, and past experiences? What work-related experience do you have that relates directly to this job?

▶ *What have you heard about this company that was of interest to you?* Focus on the company's reputation. Refer to positive publicity, media attention, or published information that caught your attention. This shows you've done your research.

▶ *What else can you tell me about yourself that isn't listed in your resume?* This is yet another opportunity for you to sell yourself to the employer. Take advantage of the opportunity.

Don't Forget to Wow 'em!

Whether or not you receive a job offer after participating in one or more interviews has nothing to do with luck. The employer's decision will be based on your skills, experience, education, and how well you present yourself and perform during the interview.

The following are strategies to help you properly prepare for an interview and make a positive first impression:

▶ The most important thing to do prior to an interview is prepare. Do research about the company you're interviewing with, the industry you'll be working in, and if possible, try to learn as much as possible about the individual who will be conducting the interview. Failure to prepare properly for each interview is a guaranteed way to stay unemployed.

▶ As part of your preparation, participate in mock interviews with a friend, relative, or career counselor. Practice answering common interview questions out loud, and compile a list of at least five intelligent questions you can ask the employer during the interview.

▶ Be sure to get a good night's sleep before the interview. You want to look and feel rested and be totally awake and alert.

▶ Before your interview, take a shower, shampoo your hair, clean your fingernails, brush your teeth, and apply antiperspirant and deodorant. Your appearance is the very first thing a potential employer is going to notice when you arrive for an interview. Making a positive first impression is critical.

▶ Make sure your interview outfit is clean, wrinkle-free, and fits you perfectly. Also, be sure your shoes are shined and coordinate well with your outfit.

▶ Make several extra copies of your resume, letters of recommendation, and your list of references and bring them to your interview. You'll also want to bring your daily planner, along with your research materials, a pad, and a working pen. All of this paperwork will fit nicely in a briefcase or portfolio. On your pad, write down the company's name, interviewer's name, address, telephone number, and directions to the location of the interview.

▶ The morning of your interview, read a local newspaper and watch a morning news program so you're aware of the day's news events and will be able to discuss them with the interviewer. Many interviewers like to start off an interview with general chitchat. You want to appear knowledgeable about what's happening in the world around you.

▶ Arrive to your interview at least 10 minutes early and check in with the receptionist. While it's okay for an interviewer to keep you, the applicant, waiting if he or she is running late, it is never appropriate for the job seeker to show up late. Next to being unprepared for the interview, arriving late is the worst mistake you can make.

▶ If you're asked to sit in a waiting room until your interview begins, use the time to compose yourself, review your research notes, and visualize yourself succeeding in the interview. In your mind, see yourself being totally calm as you answer questions in complete sentences. If you've done your preparation work, you already have an idea about what questions will be posed to you, how you plan to answer them, and what questions you want to ask the employer. Knowing that you're totally prepared for an interview, will make it easier to relax.

▶ From the moment you arrive at the interview location and step in the front door, be in interview mode. Act professionally and be polite to everyone, including secretaries and receptionists.

▶ When you're introduced to the interviewer, stand up, smile, make direct eye contact, and shake hands. Refer to the interviewer formally, as Mr./Ms./Dr. (insert last name). When you're invited to sit down, try to sit down either at the same time or after the interviewer.

▶ As the interview gets underway, sit up straight. Listen carefully to the questions posed to you. Take a moment or two to think about each answer, and then answer using complete sentences. Words like "yeah," "nope," and "umm" should not be used as part of your professional vocabulary.

▶ Throughout the entire interview, in addition to what you say, you will be evaluated based on how you conduct yourself and use body language. Prior to your interview, spend the necessary amount of time learning to control your nervous habits. If you know what your nervous habits are, they'll be easier to control in stressful situations.

▶ If, after going through the interview process, you are very interested in the position, make a point to come right out and say so. Explain exactly why you want the job, what you can offer to the company, and why you're the best candidate to fill the position.

▶ No matter what questions are asked during the interview, what the employer ultimately wants to know is if you're the best person for the job. Will you be an asset to the company if you're hired? Do you have the skills, knowledge, and experience necessary to successfully achieve the job's requirements? Will you fit nicely into the corporate culture within the company? Are you a hard worker who is dedicated and honest? Using specific examples, it's your job to convey whatever information is necessary and tell your story during an interview situation.

▶ Prior to an interview, learn as much as possible about the position you're applying for so you'll be in a better position to sell yourself as the ideal person to fill the job opening.

JOB INTERVIEWS: WHAT *NOT* TO DO

Once you get invited by a potential employer to come in for an interview, to maximize your chances of landing the job, it's critical to do everything within your power to prepare and avoid the common mistakes often made by applicants. Remember, for every job you apply for, chances are there are dozens of other applicants who'd also like to land that same job. The good news for you, however, is that there's currently a shortage of qualified people with computer skills looking to fill computer-related positions.

The following are some of the most common mistakes applicants make while preparing for or participating in job interviews, plus tips on how to avoid making these mistakes.

▶ Never lie on a resume. Don't apply for jobs you're not qualified for and then lie in order to get invited for an interview.

▶ Don't skip steps in your interview preparation. Just because you've been invited for an interview, you can't afford to wing it once you get there.

Prior to the interview, spend time doing research about the company, its products/services, and the people you'll be meeting with.

▶ Never arrive late for an interview. Arriving even five minutes late for a job interview is equivalent to telling an employer you don't want the job. The day before the interview, go to the interview location and determine exactly how to get there and how long it takes. On the day of the interview, plan on arriving at least 10 minutes early and use the restroom before you begin the actual interview.

▶ Don't neglect your appearance. First impressions are crucial. Make sure your clothing is wrinkle-free and clean, that your hair is well groomed, and that your make-up (if applicable) looks professional. Always dress up for an interview, even if the dress code at the company is casual. Also, be sure to brush your teeth prior to an interview, especially if you've eaten recently.

▶ Avoid drinking any beverages containing caffeine prior to an interview. Chances are, you'll already be nervous about the interview, and drinking coffee or soda won't calm you down.

▶ Don't go into the interview unprepared. Prior to the interview, use your research to compile a list of intelligent questions to ask the employer. These questions can be about the company, its products/services, its methods of doing business, the job responsibilities of the job you're applying for, and so on. When it's time for you to answer questions, always use complete sentences.

▶ Never bring up salary, benefits, or vacation time during the initial interview. Allow the employer to bring up the compensation package to be offered. Focus on how you (with all of your skills, experience, and education) can become a valuable asset to the company you're interviewing with.

▶ Refrain from discussing your past earning history or what you're hoping to earn. An employer typically looks for the best possible employees for the lowest possible price. Let the employer make you an offer first. When asked, tell the interviewer you're looking for a salary/benefits package that's in line with what's standard in the industry for someone with your qualifications and experience. Try to avoid stating an actual dollar figure.

▶ Avoid personal topics during the interview. There are questions that an employer can't legally ask during an interview situation or on an employment application. In addition to these topics, refrain from discussing gender, religion, politics, and any other highly personal topics.

▶ Never insult the interviewer. It's common for an interviewer to ask what you might perceive to be a stupid or irrelevant question. In some cases, the interviewer is simply testing to see how you'll respond. Some questions are asked to test your morals or determine your level of honesty. Other types of questions are used simply to see how you'll react in a tough situation. Try to avoid getting caught up in trick questions. Never tell an interview their question is stupid or irrelevant.

▶ If you're a highly trained computer specialist, don't get overly technical with the person interviewing you, unless that person is also a computer specialist. If you're interviewing with a human resources person, chances are if you start using all sorts of technical lingo, the person conducting the interview won't understand what you're talking about. If the person is the vice president of computer operations for the company, however, it's certainly appropriate to have a technical discussion during your interview.

▶ Throughout the interview, avoid allowing your body language to get out of control. For example, if you're someone who taps your foot when you're nervous, make sure you're aware of your habit so you can control it in an interview situation.

▶ If your job interview takes place over lunch or dinner, refrain from drinking alcohol of any kind.

Throughout any job interview, your primary objective should be to position yourself as the ideal candidate for the job you're applying for. By avoiding the common mistakes made by many applicants, your chances of landing a job increase dramatically. One of the best ways to prepare for an interview is to participate in mock interviews with someone who will ask you questions and then honestly critique your responses.

FOLLOW UP

After the interview, follow up with a thank-you note, e-mail, or voice mail message to the interviewer. Following up lets interviewers know that you are serious about the position and it also helps them remember you better. Here are some tips for following up:

- ▶ A thank-you note is most effective when it is written on the same day as your interview and mailed right away.
- ▶ Send a separate note to each person you interviewed with, and make each one personal. Refer to something that happened during the interview or a specific topic that was discussed.
- ▶ Check your note for spelling and grammar errors. You are trying to reinforce the impression that you are the right candidate.
- ▶ E-mail and voice mail thank-yous are sometimes appropriate, especially when you get the impression that a hiring decision is to be made very quickly, or when there are lots of candidates applying for the job. A speedy, thoughtful message may set you apart from the pack.

The business world is a cutthroat environment. People often maintain a selfish, look-out-for-themselves attitude. As a job applicant, however, this is not the attitude you want to adopt.

It's a common belief that by conducting a job interview, the interviewer is simply doing his or her job, which is to fill the position(s) the employer has available. As a result of this belief, many job seekers show no gratitude to the interviewer. Thus, a thank-you note is never sent after a job interview—and that's a mistake.

Sending a personal and well-thought-out note immediately after an interview is extremely beneficial. It will keep your name in the forefront of the hiring manager's mind. It will also show that you have good follow-up skills and that you're genuinely interested in the job opportunity. Individual and personalized thank-you notes should be sent out within 24 hours of your interview, and to everyone you met with when visiting a potential employer.

As you write the note, it should be addressed using the recipient's full name and title. Make sure you spell the person's name correctly. The note can be typewritten on personal stationery. If you choose to type your note, follow a standard business letter format.

A much more personal alternative is to hand-write your thank-you note on a professional-looking note card which can be purchased at any stationery, greeting card, or office supply store. The personal touch will add a lot to further a positive impression and help to separate you from your competition.

Keep your message brief and to the point. Thank the interviewer for taking the time out of his or her busy schedule to meet with you, and for considering you for the job opening available. Make sure you include the exact job title or position you applied for.

In one or two sentences, highlight the important details discussed in your interview. You want the interviewer to remember you. Finally, reaffirm your interest in the position and invite further contact. Keep in mind, a thank you note is never the place to discuss issues under negotiation, such as salary, benefits, concerns, work schedule, and so on.

PARTICIPATING IN INTERNSHIPS

Most colleges do an excellent job educating students, but it's impossible to teach something that virtually all employers look for—real world experience. If you're a college student, one of the best ways to jump start your career while still in school is to participate in an internship program. By working in the industry you hope to break into upon graduation, an internship will give you a chance to showcase your webmaster skills (or specific skills related to designing, programming, and managing a website).

Virtually all colleges offer structured internship programs, allowing students to work during their vacations or after classes (on a part-time basis), earn college credits, and gain valuable real world experience. Many companies, in all industries, offer paid or unpaid internship opportunities. Even if a company you want to work for doesn't offer a structured internship program, if you have direct contact with an executive within the company, it's still possible to work as an intern.

Even if participating in an internship program isn't a requirement for landing a job within the field you hope to break into, having real world experience certainly makes you a stronger and more marketable job candidate upon graduation. In addition, working as an intern provides you with incredible networking opportunities. Often, if you're able to demonstrate your abilities as an intern, you could easily transform that internship into a full-time job upon graduating. Most employers prefer to hire people who have already proven themselves to be competent and who know their company.

The best time to begin looking for internship opportunities is several months prior to when you hope to begin working. Companies with established internship programs often have an application and interview process prospective interns must complete. This is very similar to applying for a regular job and often requires submitting a resume and cover letter, along with an application, followed by participation in an interview.

If you're hoping to obtain college credit for your internship work, it's best to work through your college's internship program coordinator or one of the department heads at your school.

Before looking for an internship program to participate in, determine what your goals are. Possible goals might be to get your foot in the door at a specific company, to learn about a specific industry, to obtain real world work experience doing something that interests you, to master skills that can only be learned on-the-job (as opposed to in a classroom), to earn college credit, and/or to earn a paycheck.

As you explore specific opportunities, some of the questions you'll want to ask include:

- ▶ How many work hours are required to receive credit?
- ▶ If applicable, how much does the internship pay?
- ▶ Will you be graded for your work? If so, by a college professor or the person you work under at the company you intern for?
- ▶ Do you have to arrange your own internship with the company or work through your school?
- ▶ Does the internship program at your school also require you to attend classes, write a paper, or make a presentation to a faculty member in order to receive credit?
- ▶ What will your responsibilities be on a day-to-day basis?
- ▶ Who, within the company, will you be working for?
- ▶ Will the internship provide real world work experience that's directly related to your chosen field?
- ▶ Will your participation in the internship provide you with networking opportunities?

Once you land an internship, consider it an audition for ultimately obtaining a full-time job. Always act professionally, ask questions, follow directions, display plenty of enthusiasm, volunteer to take on additional responsibilities, meet deadlines, and work closely with your boss or supervisor. Upon graduating, make sure to highlight your internship work on your resume.

One excellent resource for finding internship opportunities—aside from personal contacts or your school—is the Internet. Vault.com Internships (www.vault.com), for example, offers a listing of internships available nationwide.

The following books are also excellent resources:

▶ *Internship Success* by Marianne Ehrlich Green (VGM Career Horizons, $12.95)
▶ *Peterson's 2000 Internships* (Petersons Guides, $24.95)
▶ *America's Top Internships, 2000 Edition* by Mark Oldman (Princeton Review, $21.00)
▶ *The Yale Daily News Guide to Internships 2000* by John Anselmi (Kaplan, $25.00)

As you can see, there are many steps involved in finding, applying for, and landing a job. Throughout this entire process, make sure you keep a positive attitude, put in the time necessary to complete each step of the process properly, and that you never lose focus on what you're trying to accomplish—finding the best possible job opportunity for yourself. Once you have the necessary training in the computer field, you'll find that many exciting job opportunities will be open to you. Your goal should be to find the job opportunity that meets your own needs and desires. Never simply settle for the first job that comes along.

THE INSIDE TRACK

Who: Mike Harp

What: Director of Technology

Where: FANSOnly Network

INSIDER'S STORY

I started out in the publishing industry—magazines, specifically. I did desktop publishing, was involved in networking systems, and had some design background. A few years into my publishing career I decided that I wanted to do something involving the Internet because it was new and exciting. At the time (the early- to mid-90s), graphic artists in the magazine industry became a dime a dozen. I wanted to specialize in something different.

I spent two years in Web consulting before this job—it was kind of a transition period. When I started here, the company was really small, and I was a developer *and* graphic artist.

My current job involves handling the administrative software of the company. I deal with things like ad serving, traffic management, and architectural development. We use open source software, and we often need to modify it to suit our needs.

One of my recent projects was to develop a live game application that needed to handle 2.5 million page requests per hour. We needed a radically different architecture than we had been using. I came up with the specs for the project, and modified the open source software to meet those specs.

This field is definitely very challenging. If you don't stay in a mode where you're continually learning new talents, but instead only rely on your existing abilities, you'll get left behind. From one day to the next, it's never really boring. I like the team we've assembled here, and we always challenge each other to do things better.

INSIDER'S ADVICE

Anyone wanting to get into this business needs to have a good attitude. When we hire people, degrees and certificates only go so far—like MSC certificates—everyone has one of those. They help, but what we really look for is an attitude that you really want to learn and be part of the team. And if you don't know something, you should have the attitude that you think it'll be really cool to figure the problem out.

CHAPTER seven

HOW TO SUCCEED ONCE YOU'VE LANDED THE JOB

BY FOLLOWING the advice offered in earlier chapters, it's likely that you'll be landing an exciting job as a webmaster or elsewhere in the IT field. This job should be one that you'll thoroughly enjoy and that will lead you toward future career advancement. From this chapter, you'll discover valuable secrets for surviving and thriving in your new career. You'll learn about managing important work relationships, how to better fit into the workplace culture, how to manage your time, find a mentor, and make your mark while on the job.

MANAGING WORK RELATIONSHIPS: BASIC RULES

From the moment you begin applying for jobs and participating in job interviews, you are establishing and building your professional reputation. This reputation is what people think of you in terms of your personality, competence, and attitude. This perception contributes greatly to what co-workers, subordinates, managers, clients, customers, and anyone else you come into professional contact with, might say or think about you behind your back.

No matter what type of career you choose to pursue, especially one in the IT field, your success will depend largely on the business relationships you develop and cultivate. Making a conscious effort to respect others, become a "people person," and make sure you're a "team player" while on the job will help your career immensely.

When it comes to building and maintaining professional relationships, some basic rules apply to any workplace.

Sometimes Peace Is Better Than Justice

You may be absolutely 100% sure you are right about a specific situation. Unfortunately, you may have coworkers who doubt you or who flatly disagree with you. This is a common occurrence in the workplace.

In some situations, you need to assert your position and convince the disbelievers to trust your judgment. Your previous track record and reputation will go a long way in helping to convince people to trust your opinions, ideas, and decisions. However, carefully consider the gravity of the situation before you stick your neck out.

In other words, in a work environment, choose your battles wisely. For instance, go ahead and argue your position if you can prevent a catastrophe. On the other hand, if you are having a debate about an issue of taste, opinion, or preference, you may want to leave the situation alone or accept the decisions of your superiors. Let your recommendations be known, but do not argue your point relentlessly. Sometimes you will be right and people will not listen to you. Always be open to compromise and be willing to listen to and consider the options and ideas of others.

Don't Burn Bridges

If you are in a disagreement, if you are leaving one employment situation for another, or if a project is ending, always leave the work relationship on a good note. Remember, your professional reputation will follow you throughout your career. It will take years to build a positive reputation, but only one mistake could destroy it.

When changing jobs, don't take the opportunity to speak your mind in a ranting and raving manner before you leave. While it might make you feel good for about three minutes, it will have a lasting effect on your career and on people's perception of you. Someone with whom you have negative interactions could become your boss someday or might be able to help you down the line. No matter what industry you ultimately work in, you'll find that it's probably a close-knit community and that people know each other—either in person or by reputation.

If you wind up acting unprofessionally toward someone, even if you don't ever have contact with that person again, he or she will have contact with many other people and possibly describe you as hard to work with or downright rude. Your work reputation is very important; don't tarnish it by burning your bridges.

Likewise, when changing employment situations, do so in a professional manner. There are countless reasons why someone leaves one job to pursue a career with another company, but to maintain a good reputation within an industry, it's important to act professionally when you actually quit a job. Getting into a fight with your boss, shouting, "I quit!" and then stomping out of the building forever is never the best way to handle things. Never let your negative feelings cause you to act unprofessionally.

If you get into a major disagreement with your employer, never make a decision to quit impulsively. Spend a few days thinking about your decision, and if you decide it's time to move on, start looking for a new job before actually tendering your resignation with your current employer. As a general rule, even if you're not getting along with your boss or coworkers, it's not a good idea to quit your current job until you've lined up a new one.

Once you've actually landed that new job, be prepared to give your current employer the traditional two weeks notice. Some people give notice and then use their accumulated vacation or sick days to avoid showing up for work. This behavior is not appropriate. Even if your new employer wants you to start work immediately, they will almost always understand that as a matter of loyalty and professional courtesy, it is necessary for you to stay with your current employer for those two weeks after giving your notice.

During those last two weeks on the job, offer to do whatever you can to maintain a positive relationship with your coworkers and boss, such as offering to train your replacement. Make your exit from the company as smooth as possible. Purposely causing problems, stealing from the employer, or sabotaging business deals are all actions that are unethical and totally inappropriate. Some companies will request your immediate departure when you quit, and will cut off your computer access and escort you out of the building, especially if you're leaving on a negative note. Prior to quitting, try to determine how past colleagues were treated, so you'll know what to expect.

As you actually leave the company for the last time, take with you only your personal belongings and nothing that is considered the company's property. Make a point to return, directly to your boss, your office keys and any company-owned equipment that was in your possession. If possible, for your protection, obtain a written memo stating that everything was returned promptly and in working order.

Bear in mind that you might need to use your current employer as a reference down the road. Simply walking off the job and leaving your department in a bind is not the best way to maintain positive relationships.

When you're actually ready to quit your current job, arrange a private meeting with your boss or with the appropriate person within the company, and offer your resignation in-person, following it up in writing with a friendly and professional letter.

Keep Work and Your Social Life Separate

You were hired to do a job, not to meet new friends and potential dates. While it's important to be friendly and form positive relationships with the people you work with, beware of becoming too chummy. Personal relationships can wreak havoc in the workplace, especially if those relationships become romantic. Consider that you might have to rate a friend's job performance, take work direction from a buddy, or fire someone you hang out with. While there are challenges associated with working with friends, these can often be handled professionally. The challenges associated with at-work romances, however, more often than not lead to disaster.

MANAGING RELATIONSHIPS WITH YOUR COWORKERS

You will meet many people in the course of your career. Some you will admire; some you will find barely tolerable. For your personal development, you need to find a way to work well with everyone—even if they're not your best friends. Acknowledging and accepting someone else's talents and expertise is very different from being their close friend, yet in the workplace, maintaining a professional respect for people you work with will allow everyone to be more productive and successful.

The following are some fundamental rules for fostering positive working relationships with your peers:

▶ Don't gossip about your boss, your coworkers, or anyone else. Gossip hurts the person being talked about, will inevitably come back to haunt you, and also can make you look like you don't have enough to do.

▶ Foster sharing relationships instead of competitive relationships. If you experiment with a great new piece of software or read an interesting article in a computer magazine, share the information with your coworkers. A group of people who help each other develop professionally will shine as a team and as individuals. On the other hand, if you jockey for position and compete over everything, you will miss out on the wealth that you could learn from your coworkers—and will have to live in a strained work environment.

▶ Don't become known as a "Long Ranger"—looking out only for yourself. Especially when it comes time for employee evaluations or being considered for a raise or promotion, you want to be considered a hard working, sincere, honest, "team player" who does his or her best work in the interest of the company as a whole.

MANAGING YOUR RELATIONSHIP WITH YOUR BOSS

Depending on your boss, this relationship can be pleasurable or painful. In any case, it's important to keep the communication lines open. Talk to your boss about his or her management style and adjust your expectations to work within that style. For instance, your first boss might like to be hands-on and help you trouble-shoot problems. She might want to talk to you at least once a day to hear about your activities. You need to understand that this boss wants to empower you through a mentoring/teaching style.

On the other hand, your boss might want you to call him only if you have a problem and simply submit a weekly status report on your projects. You need to understand that this boss wants to empower you through a hands-off style that lets you find your own solutions. Both bosses may be good managers; they simply have different styles. Understand the value of each style and get the most from it.

Also talk to your boss about *your* career goals. Set goals for six months, one year, three years, and five years. Based on your discussions, you and your boss can create projects and strategies to lead you toward your goals. If you are a people person and an organizer, you might want to move toward a management position and set relevant goals. No matter what you are interested in, make a plan, share it with your boss, and get a few steps closer to achieving your goals.

Dealing with a Difficult Boss

If you're in a situation where you simply don't see eye-to-eye with your boss, you have several options. You can do nothing, hoping that it doesn't get worse, and not let your relationship with your boss impact you emotionally, or you can quit your job and seek employment elsewhere. Either of these might appear to be the easiest solution to your problem, but neither will most likely lead to long-term career fulfillment.

Another option is to carefully evaluate your situation and choose to alter your attitude and behavior, and to do whatever it takes to develop a relationship with your boss that evolves around mutual respect. Developing this type of professional relationship doesn't mean you'll become best friends with your boss, but it does mean that you should find a way to work together so that you're both happy and productive.

Dealing with a difficult boss who acts unprofessionally or childishly, and attacks or criticizes you in front of your peers can be extremely difficult. The worst mistake you can make in this situation is allowing yourself to drop to his or her level. This behavior will only intensify the situation, creating a more stressful work environment. Developing a relationship with a boss that's based upon mutual respect is critical, which means it'll probably be necessary to confront your boss.

As you prepare to confront your boss, ask yourself if you're being singled out by his or her unprofessional behavior, or if your boss treats everyone poorly. Prior to an actual confrontation, try to determine the core reasons for your boss's behavior. Do your intelligence, capabilities, and potential threaten him or her? Is your boss bullying you because he or she is filled with self-doubt and insecurity? Does your boss simply lack good management or communication skills? Is your boss such a control freak that anything anyone else does is wrong?

Once you understand the true reasons for your boss' actions and behavior, you'll be in a much better position to deal with it in a highly professional manner. If your boss is a bully, he or she expects his or her subordinates to be spineless followers. By simply standing up for yourself, making direct eye contact with your boss and standing or sitting up straight when in their presence, you will be in a much better position to earn their respect. Without being overly aggressive or rude, make it clear that you expect respect from your superior.

Bosses who are controlling often lack the ability to trust others. Thus, to make your situation more bearable, your goal should be to build trust between yourself and your boss. This will require exceeding their expectations and performing with a high level of efficiency over time. Demonstrate that you respect your boss' opinion and knowledge, and take some time to build your own autonomy in the workplace.

One of the worst situations is when a boss is untrustworthy or unethical in the way they perform their job. In this case, watch your back carefully. Be sure that you document all of your work and accomplishments. When dealing directly with your boss, make sure that other people are present, and never agree to do anything that might jeopardize your reputation or job. If your boss's actions are illegal or highly unethical, it might be necessary to take measures in order to protect yourself and your career.

When dealing with a difficult boss, try your best to remain calm. Use direct eye contact and confident body language to convey your professional attitude. Don't assume you can work hard to change someone else, because you can't. You'll wind up wasting your time and energy. If you choose to accept the situation, set boundaries and then object when your boss goes beyond those boundaries. If a particular situation becomes too intense, take a break, walk away, and let yourself cool down. Often, if you can determine why your boss is acting the way he or she is, you'll be able to find easy ways to lighten the situation. Prior to confronting your boss, make sure that your problems aren't a result of your own attitude or behavior.

Having an occasional disagreement with a manager is normal, but if your work life is being compromised by the actions of a mean or difficult boss, it's up to you to take action and find a solution that works for you.

FITTING INTO THE WORKPLACE CULTURE

Workplace cultures can vary widely even within the same industry. A company's culture can be formal and stiff, relaxed and casual, or somewhere in between. The three main types of corporate cultures are: entrepreneurial, small business, and corporate.

An entrepreneurial culture emphasizes risk taking and working independently. Employees tend to wear many hats and are given a wide range of responsibilities. Entrepreneurial cultures often admire and reward a well-presented, flashy, and stylish idea. You are selling your idea, and the sale requires some pizzazz. Entrepreneurial cultures often are competitive; they are frequently in quick, big-money fields and often pay on commission. The advantage of entrepreneurial cultures, of course, is that they often pay well. The disadvantage is the overly competitive and stressful atmosphere.

Despite the name, small business cultures are not always found in small companies. While entrepreneurial cultures are competitive, small business cultures are more relaxed and informal. They often nurture as many new ideas as any other type of workplace, but they don't have such a competitive edge. This team culture is more of a cooperative, brainstorming, think-tank environment. If one person is successful, everyone shares the success. The advantage of this type of culture is that it fosters a pleasant working environment that promotes growth and cooperation. The disadvantage is that jobs in this environment often do not pay as much as in other cultures.

The third workplace culture is corporate. This culture relies on a reporting structure and hierarchy to accomplish defined goals. Many large companies adopt this style simply because they have a large number of people to manage. One manager (or president or vice president) cannot talk to everyone in the company all the time about his or her ideas. Instead, there's a functional reporting system. You might have a president, who has seven vice presidents, who each has seven directors, who each has seven managers, one of whom has you and several coworkers in his or her reporting chain. For employees, the advantage in this type of culture is usually job security, the availability of additional training (often company paid), and a good, long-term salary. The disadvantage is that employees do not have as much freedom as in other cultures and may have to spend more time writing reports and filling out forms than others. In a highly corporate culture, job titles are clearly defined, there is a predefined path to follow for raises and promotions, and there is little opportunity for an employee to shine outside of his or her own defined job.

There is no perfect workplace culture. You need to find one that suits your needs. Do you want financial security and continued training? Then go for a large corporate environment. Are you willing to put in a lot of hours for quick money? Then pursue an entrepreneurial culture. Are you searching for a cooperative, stable working environment? Then a small company culture is probably right for you.

You may think you would not fit into certain cultures, but try not to discount anything off hand. Decide which you think will be the best fit and try it; but remain willing to try another culture if a great opportunity arises.

MANAGING YOUR TIME

You'll most likely find that the workplace environment is more hectic than school was, so you will need to manage your time effectively to make the most of your work week. Here are some tips for juggling your tasks and managing your time.

Daily Work Activities

1. *Know the requirements of your job and what your boss expects of you.* Define your role and know what you are expected to deliver on a daily basis.
2. *Don't get trapped by interruptions and time wasters.* Every job is subject to time wasters. Sometimes you may get caught up by people who want to chat socially; or you may fall into the trap of playing computer games or reading the news. It is important to allow yourself a small amount of relaxation throughout the day, but set limits for yourself—

such as 15 minutes per day—so it doesn't get out of control. If you work with a social, chatty person, don't let yourself be distracted or interrupted. If you are working on something, let your coworker know that you are busy and can perhaps talk later, during lunch. If you do have time to talk to your coworker, try to steer the conversation to computer-related topics. Use the time to learn something new from your coworker rather than just chat.

3. *Keep a day planner.* Identify one place where you write everything down, whether it is a formal day planner or a spiral notebook. Are you always running late for appointments? Do the items on your daily to-do list never seem to get done fast enough? If there is never enough time in your day to meet your personal and professional obligations, you could be lacking important time management skills.

Learning time management skills won't add more hours to the work day, but it will allow you to use all of your time more productively, reduce the stress in your life, better focus on what's important, and ultimately get more done faster. Time management is easy to learn and requires just one basic tool—a daily planner, personal digital assistant, or specialized scheduling software for your computer.

Once you obtain a time management tool, spend several days carefully analyzing how you spend every minute of your day. Determine what takes up the majority of your time, but diminishes your productivity. Perhaps you experience countless interruptions from coworkers or long telephone calls; you don't have well-defined priorities; your work area is messy and disorganized; you have too much to do and become overwhelmed; or you're constantly forced to participate in unscheduled meetings. As you examine how you spend your day, pinpoint the biggest time wasters that are keeping your from getting your most important work done.

Take major projects, goals, and objectives and divide them into smaller, more manageable tasks. You'll need to incorporate your to-do list into your daily planner, allowing you to schedule your time. Make sure you attempt to complete your high-priority items and tasks early in the day, giving those items your full attention. Also, make sure you list all of your prescheduled appointments in your daily schedule, allowing ample time to get to and from the appointments, and if necessary, prepare for them in advance.

Once you commit to using a time management tool, it's important to remain disciplined and use it continually until it becomes second nature. Initially, you may have to spend up to 30 minutes per day planning your time and creating your to-do list, but ultimately, you'll begin saving up to several hours per day. Learning to better manage your time will boost your productivity, which will ultimately make you more valuable to an employer, putting you in a better position to eventually receive a raise or promotion.

MANAGING LIFE AND A JOB

When you are at work every day all week long, it becomes difficult to get your life tasks done. Here are some tips to help you integrate your job with your life.

▶ Make to-do lists and prioritize the tasks you need to accomplish. Keep a list of things you need to buy, return, pick up, and drop off. A day planner is the best place to keep such a list. If you don't have a day planner, carry a notebook with you from home to work and back again. Organize your list according to places you will stop. Keep grocery items on one list, pharmacy items on another, dry cleaning on a third, and so on. Cross things off the lists when you have finished them so you can see what you have to do at a glance.

▶ Use your lunch hour to run errands at least once a week. Identify resources that are close to your work for things you can do during this time—doctor, dentist, dry cleaner, shoe repair, car repair, hardware store, and so on.

▶ Use the commute between home and work to take care of other errands, such as stopping at the pharmacy and the grocery store.

FINDING A MENTOR

A mentor is someone you identify as successful and with whom you create a teacher–student relationship. Choose your mentor based on what is important to you and on how you define success. Someone can be successful without having attained certain titles or positions, so keep an open mind when you're looking for a mentor. A mentor is someone you can learn from. Enter into the relationship intending to observe your mentor carefully and ask many questions.

There are two primary types of mentors: a business mentor and a technical mentor. A business mentor will provide guidance about how to be successful in the business culture.

Although each mentoring situation is different, you often can learn the following from a business mentor:

▶ customer service skills
▶ presentation skills
▶ how to design a career plan
▶ how to set incremental goals
▶ what to expect in your business culture
▶ how to communicate with your boss
▶ how to gain sponsorship for your ideas

A technical mentor, on the other hand, is someone who has more technical knowledge than you do and can teach you those skills, direct your path for ongoing learning, and help you develop technical problem-solving skills. You often can learn the following from a technical mentor:

▶ problem-solving skills
▶ in-depth knowledge about technology used by your company
▶ tricks and shortcuts for repair and maintenance
▶ trends in technology
▶ which computer magazines are best
▶ which conferences/seminars/classes you should attend

How to Connect with a Mentor

Don't just wait for your fairy godmother to appear and provide you with a mentor; actively search for one! A mentor can be anyone from a senior-level manager to one of your peers. Remember, finding a good mentor is not a matter of title, years in the business, or years with your company. A good mentor is someone who is expert in a certain area and willing and able to teach you.

There are many ways to find a mentor. Since you probably will be looking for a mentor when you start your new job, you won't know many people at the company. Try these techniques for identifying possible mentors:

▶ Ask your boss to recommend someone. Let your supervisor know that you are proactively trying to improve yourself through a mentor. This actually helps you in two ways. First, it helps you find an appropriate mentor based on your boss' experience at the company and in the industry. Second, it lets your boss know that you are serious about your career and your personal development.

▶ Observe people. You can learn a lot this way. When asked a question, do they take the time to help you find a resolution or do they point you toward someone else who can help you? The one who takes the time to help you resolve your problem is the better choice for a mentor. How does the potential mentor resolve problems? In a calm manner? Do problems get resolved? If so, you've found a good candidate.

▶ Listen to people who admire your potential mentor. What qualities do they admire? Do the admirable qualities coincide with your values and goals? If you need to learn conflict-resolution skills, you probably shouldn't consider a mentor who is admired for a forceful, aggressive style. Instead, look for someone people describe as fair, calm, and easy to work with.

SURVIVING YOUR FIRST WEEKS AT A NEW JOB

For many job seekers, the stress involved with finding new job opportunities, sending out resumes, participating in interviews, and dealing with all of the other hassles involved with finding employment can be emotionally draining. Thus, it makes perfect sense that most people experience a huge sense of relief once they're actually offered a new job, conduct a successful salary negotiation, and then accept a new position.

The problem is, as soon as some people show up for their first day of work, the stress associated with beginning a new job kicks in, which could make the first few weeks at a new job unpleasant. Stepping into a new job situation can be difficult. It often involves a major change in your daily routine, getting to know an entirely new group of people, and learning the policies and procedures of your new employer.

You also need to learn about the underlying office politics that play a major role in any work environment, and determine exactly what is expected of you in terms of job performance. It's necessary to determine exactly how your position fits into the overall operation of the company and be willing to adapt your work habits to meet the needs of the employer.

Starting a new job may also require you to learn new skills or force you to step into a high-pressure situation and immediately perform at your peak efficiency, even before you're given a proper new employee orientation. While stepping into a new job means a major change in your life, it also impacts your new coworkers, who might feel threatened by you and not immediately accept you as a peer. Sometimes, your new colleagues may take out on you their discomfort of having to deal with change as well as their own frustrations with their job.

One of the best things you can do before showing up for your first day of work is research. If possible, try to schedule an appointment, in advance, to meet your immediate superiors and coworkers and receive a tour of your work environment.

Hopefully, before accepting a new job, you did the necessary research to learn about the company and position, and you're now confident you've found a job that will allow you to combine your interests, skills, and educational background. If you go into a new job knowing there's a good chance you're going to enjoy it, the stress associated with starting the job will be greatly diminished, since much of the stress you'd typically feel would be in anticipation of entering into an unknown situation.

Adapting to a new work situation happens instantaneously for some, but for others could take up to three or four weeks. During this time, be open-minded and try to maintain a positive attitude, no matter how unhappy or stressed out you are. Until some time has passed, it's difficult to tell if you simply accepted the wrong job, or if you're experiencing the normal new job acclimation process. Unless you're absolutely sure you've made the wrong job decision after a week or two, stick it out for at least a month before making the decision to quit.

During your first few weeks at a new job, there are several things you can do to help yourself and your coworkers become more comfortable. First, instead of confronting people who may give you a difficult time, try to fit in right from the start by being friendly toward everyone. Also, ask questions to demonstrate a desire to learn how things are done, and whenever possible, attempt to strike up nonwork-related conversations, especially during lunch or break periods. This will help you get to know the people you're working with on a personal level.

If your job requires you to learn new skills, understand that anytime someone attempts to learn something new it'll take time, effort, and patience. Even if you received top grades in school, actually learning to put your textbook knowledge to work in the real world is a learning process unto itself. In order to meet the expectations of your employer, be prepared to put in some extra hours initially, as you learn how to perform in your new job and master the skills required to fulfill the job's responsibilities.

Middle- and large-sized companies tend to hire groups of people at the same time and put them through the same new employee orientation process and training. As you meet your new coworkers who are beginning their jobs at the same time as you, keep in mind they're in the same situation as you are. Try to develop a friendship with these people early on during your orientation or training, so when you actually begin working, you won't be entering a new job situation alone.

Always think of a new job as providing a new set of exciting opportunities and a chance to start fresh. By taking control of your life, you can seek out and pursue those opportunities that will lead to career advancement and happiness. You must, however, face these opportunities with the proper mind-set and be willing to work hard for what you want. Never allow the fear of failure to hold you back as you begin to take advantage of the opportunities your new job has to offer.

Finally, some jobs, especially those involving sales, take time before you will begin to achieve positive results. After all, it's necessary to get to know the product or service you're selling and develop your own client list. Depending on what you're selling, the actual sales cycle could be a few weeks or several months, so be patient and persistent. Many real estate agents, for example, say it takes up to one year on the job before you can expect to receive a steady income based on commissions.

If you begin your new job determined to be open minded, professional, friendly, persistent, and flexible, chances are you'll adapt quickly and soon be accepted by your new coworkers.

A FEW FINAL THOUGHTS

From this book, you hopefully discovered that the webmaster and information technology fields offer a wide range of career opportunities in virtually every industry. Furthermore, you discovered some of the many career paths open to qualified webmasters and those interested in jobs relating to the Internet. While there are an abundance of jobs available in America for trained IT professionals and webmasters with the skills that are in demand, if you're willing to work overseas, keep in mind that the foreign job market offers even greater opportunities.

Once you've landed a job in the IT field, never stop pursuing new knowledge and training. Keeping up with the latest Internet technologies, software, Web browsers, operating systems, programming techniques, and hardware will ensure that you continue to be a valuable asset to your employer. You'll be worth more as an employee, be more easily promotable, and have greater earning potential. Be sure to take training courses, read technical manuals, read computer magazines, attend special interest group meetings, attend trade shows, and talk with other people in your field as often as possible.

We're at the dawn of the 21st century. Companies and individuals alike are becoming more and more dependant on computers, technology, and the Internet. This trend shows no signs of changing, which means the job opportunities for people with the power to utilize the Web will be plentiful both now and in the future.

THE INSIDE TRACK

Who: Ariel Rey

What: Director of Production

Where: FOXNEWS.COM

INSIDER'S STORY

I got my start in technology working in Sales Communication at a publishing company. This was around the time that the term "intranet" was being bandied about. So, I decided to learn HTML (I used *Learn HTML in 14 Days,* which I read in four). Then, with the help of an intern, I built an intranet that eventually turned into a massive repository of sales information. I was hooked on technology from that point.

To hone my skills, most of my learning was done online and by reading. Later, I took some supplemental adult education classes, primarily on programming (C, Java).

What I really like about this field is the innovation—the way it's constantly and quickly evolving. The past few years it's felt like there's been tremendous innovation. It never seems to stop.

My current role is Director of Production and Development. I oversee the general production and operation of my company's site. In other words, if it's broken, I fix it. One of my biggest tasks right now is to bring a content management and publishing system online, which has required a lot of time and effort. I have a team of producers and programmers who develop special interactive projects as well. I do plenty of research, and regularly talk to vendors about additional tools to expand the functionality of the site.

INSIDER'S ADVICE

My advice for anyone who wants to get into this field is this: Read *everything!* Stay up to date on the latest trends. Learn HTML. (Yes, it's still important). Understand XML and what it can do for your business. Look to broadband, but remember that everyday use is still a few years away.

Appendix A

Professional Associations

WEBMASTER-RELATED PROFESSIONAL ASSOCIATIONS

Association for Information Systems
P.O. Box 2712
Atlanta, GA 30301-2712
404-651-0258
Fax: 404-651-4938
E-mail: ais@gsu.edu
www.aisnet.org

Association of African American Web
Developers
E-mail: admin@aaawd.org
www.aaawd.org

Association of Information Technology
Professionals
315 South Northwest Highway, Suite 200
Park Ridge, IL 60068-4278
847-825-8124 or 800-224-9371
Fax: 847-825-1693
E-mail: aitp_hq@aitp.org
www.aitp.org

Association of Internet Professionals
The Empire State Building
350 Fifth Avenue
Suite 3018
New York, NY 10118
877-AIP-0800
E-mail: membership@association.org
www.association.org

Association of Information Technology
Professionals (AITP)
505 Busse Highway
Park Ridge, IL 60068
800-224-9371 x242
www.aitp.org

Association of Web Professionals
901 N. Pitt Street, Suite 200
Alexandria, VA 22314
888-463-6297
E-mail: dkwasnicki@a-w-p.org
www.a-w-p.org

Association for Women in Computing
41 Sutter Street, Suite 1006
San Francisco, CA 94104
415-979-8450
E-mail: awc-sf@pobox.com
www.awc-hq.org

Computer Professionals for Social
Responsibility (CPSR)
P.O. Box 717
Palo Alto, CA 94302
650-322-3778
Fax: 650-322-4748
www.cpsr.org/dox/home.html

Electronic Frontier Foundation
454 Shotwell Street
San Francisco, CA 94110-1914
415-436-9333
Fax: 415-436-9993
E-mail: info@eff.org
www.eff.org

Information Technology Association of
America 1401 Wilson Boulevard
Suite 1100
Arlington, VA 22209
703-522-5055
Fax: 703-525-2279
www.itaa.org

Information Technology Industry Council
1250 Eye Street NW, Suite 200
Washington, DC 20005
202-737-8888
Fax: 202-638-4922
E-mail: webmaster@itic.org
www.itic.org

HTML Writers Guild
E-mail: membership-questions@hwg.org
www.hwg.org

Information Systems Consultant's
Association (ISCA)
P.O. Box 467190
Atlanta, GA 30346
800-832-7767 or 770-491-1500
Fax: 770-491-3600
E-mail: president@isca.org
www.isca.org

International Alliance of Web Developers
(IAWD)
7601 Livingston Road, First Floor
Oxon Hill, MD 20745
301-749-9436
E-mail: info@iawd.org
www.iawd.org

International Association of Web Masters
and Designers
13833-E4 Wellington Trace
PMB Suite #214
Wellington, FL 33414
561-533-9008 or 509-463-6311
E-mail: support@mailbox.iawmd.com
www.iawmd.com

International Council of Online
Professionals™
2475 Robb Drive
Suite 1614
Reno, NV 89523
775-624-1502
E-mail: jlscott@i-cop.org
www.i-cop.org

International Webmasters Association
119 East Union Street
Suite E
Pasadena, CA 91103
626-449-3709
Fax: 626-449-8308
www.iwanet.org

Library & Information Technology
Association (LITA)
American Library Association
50 East Huron Street
Chicago, IL 60611-2795
800-545-2433 x4270
Fax: 312-280-3257
E-mail: lita@ala.org
www.lita.org

Network Professional Association (NPA)
195 C Street, Suite 250
Tustin, CA 92780
714-573-4780
Fax: 714-669-9341
E-mail: npa@npa.org
www.npa.org

Society for Information Management
401 North Michigan Avenue
Chicago, IL 60611-4267
800-387-9746
Fax: 312-245-1081
E-mail: info@simnet.org
www.simnet.org

The U.S. Internet Industry Association
919 18th Street, 10th Floor
Washington, DC 20006
202-496-9007
Fax: 202-496-9020
E-mail: info@usiia.org
www.usiia.org

Webgrrls International
The Woman's Techknowledge Connection
Lenox Hill Station
P.O. Box 2425
New York, NY 10021
E-mail: webgrrls@cgim.com
www.webgrrls.com

World Information Technology and Services
Alliance
8300 Boone Boulevard, Suite 450
Vienna, VA 22182
703-284-5329
E-mail: kclaman@itaa.org
www.witsa.org

World Organization of Webmasters
9580 Oak Avenue Parkway, Suite 7–177
Folsom, CA 95630
916-608-1597
Fax: 916-987-3022
E-mail: info@joinwow.org
www.joinwow.org

Web Design and Developers Association
(WDDA)
8515 Brower Street
Houston, TX 77017
435-518-9784
E-mail: wdda@wdda.org
www.wdda.org

Appendix B

Additional Resources

COLLEGES AND FINANCIAL AID

Best 331 Colleges: 2001 Edition. (Princeton, NJ: Princeton Review, 2001).

Cassidy, Daniel J. *The Scholarship Book 2001: The Complete Guide to Private-Sector Scholarships, Fellowships, Grants, and Loans for the Undergraduate* (New York: Prentice-Hall, 2001).

Kaplan Guide to the Best Colleges in the U.S. 2001. (New York: Kaplan Publishing, 2001).

Occupational Outlook Handbook. (Washington, DC: U.S. Department of Labor, 2001).

Peterson's Guide to Two-Year Colleges 1998: The Only Guide to More than 1,500 Community and Junior Colleges. (Princeton, NJ: Peterson's Guides, 1998).

Peterson's Guide to Colleges for Careers in Computing. (Princeton, NJ: Peterson's Guides, 1996).

The College Board College Cost & Financial Aid Handbook 2001. (New York: College Entrance Examination Board, 2001).

The College Board Index of Majors and Graduate Degrees 2001. (New York: College Entrance Examination Board, 2001).

CAREER-RELATED PRINT RESOURCES

Bower, Marty et al. *Web Programming Languages SourceBook: Just What a Webmaster Needs to Know About: Perl, UNIX Shell Languages, Java, JavaScript, VBScript . . .* (New York: John Wiley & Sons, Incorporated, 1997).

Ditto, Christopher. *WebMaster Answers! Certified Tech Support.* (New York: Osborne/McGraw-Hill, 1998).

Gerend, Jason, and Stephen L. Nelson. *New Webmaster's Guide to Frontpage 2001.* (Redmond, WA: Redmond Technology, Inc., 2001).

Gutierrez, Dan D. *Web Database Development for Windows Platforms.* (New York: Prentice-Hall, 1999).

Homer, Alex. *Professional ASP Techniques for Webmasters.* (Chicago: Wrox Press, Inc., 1998).

Kienan, Brenda, and Daniel Tauber. *Webmastering for Dummies.* (New York: Hungry Minds, Incorporated, 2000).

Marckini, Fredrick W. *Webmaster's Guide to Search Engine Positioning.* (Plano, TX: Wordware Publishing, Inc., 1999).

McCormack, Joe. *Webmaster's Guru Pack.* (San Diego: MnetWeb Services, 1999).

Spainhour, Stephen, et al. *Webmaster in a Nutshell.* (Cambridge, MA: O'Reilly & Associates, Incorporated, 1999).

DESIGN

Bos, Bert, and Hakon Wium Lie. *Cascading Style Sheets: Designing for the Web 2nd Edition.* (New York: Addison Wesley Longman, Inc., 1999).

Brinck, Tom. *Designing Highly Usable Web Sites.* (San Francisco, CA: Morgan Kaufmann Publishers, 2001).

Fleming, Jennifer. *Web Navigation: Designing the User Experience.* (Cambridge, MA: O'Reilly & Associates, Incorporated, 1998).

Niederst, Jen. *Designing for the Web* (Cambridge, MA: O'Reilly & Associates, Inc., 2000).

Veen, Jeffrey. *The Art and Science of Web Design.* (Indianapolis, IN: Macmillan/Query, 2000).

Weinman, Gary et al. *Creative HTML Design.2: A Hands-on HTML 4.0 Web Design Tutorial with CDROM.* (Indianapolis, IN: New Riders Publishing, 2001).

HTML

ActiveEducation's Introduction to HTML (Golden, CO: ActiveEducation, 2000).

Carey, Joan, and Patrick Carey. *Creating Web Pages with HTML: Comprehensive*, 2nd Edition (New York: Course Technology, Inc., 2000).

Castro, Elizabeth. *HTML for the World Wide Web: Visual QuickStart Guide*, 4th Edition (Berkeley, CA: Peachpit Press, 1999).

Evans, Tim. *10 Minute Guide to HTML*, 2nd Edition (Cambridge, MA: Macmillan/Que, 1996).

Klein, Jeannine M. *Building Enhanced HTML Help with Dhtml and CSS.* (New York: Prentice-Hall, 2000).

Schengili-Roberts, Keith, and Kim Silk-Copeland. *The Advanced HTML Companion*, 2nd Edition (San Diego, CA: Academic Press, Incorporated, 1998).

Taylor, Dave. *Creating Cool HTML 4 Web Pages*, 2nd Edition (New York: Hungry Minds, Incorporated, 2000).

JAVA

Ernest, Michael. *Complete Java 2 Certification Study Guide with CD-ROM.* (Alameda, CA: Sybex, Incorporated, 2000).

Java 2 Certification Virtual (Alameda, CA: Sybex, Incorporated, 2000).

Maione, Dennis. *Java 2 Programmer's Certification Bible with CD-ROM* (New York: Hungry Minds, Incorporated, 2001).

Roberts, S. *Java 2 Certification Virtual Trainer* (Alameda, CA: Sytex, 2001).

Mughal, Khalid Azim, and Rolf W. Rasmussen. *A Programmer's Guide to Java Certification: A Comprehensive Primer* (New York: Addison Wesley Longman, Inc., 1999).

JAVASCRIPT

Negrino, Tom, and Dori Smith. *JavaScript for the World Wide Web* (Berkeley, CA: Peachpit Press, 1999).

MICROSOFT

Barber, Maryann. *Exploring Microsoft Office Professional 2000: Proficient Certification* (New York: Prentice-Hall, 1999).

Iseminger, David. *Microsoft Network Services Developer's Reference Library* (Redmond, WA: Microsoft Press, 2000).

Jeansonne, William C. *Microsoft Certification Careers: Earn More Money* (New York: Hungry Minds, Incorporated, 1999).

Meinster, Barry. *Microsoft Windows NT 4.0 : Getting Started* (Cincinnati, OH: South-Western Publishing Company, 1998).

Miller, Joyce. *Preparing for Mous Certification Microsoft Access 2000* (New York: DDC Publishing, 2000).

Preparing for Microsoft Windows 2000 Professional Mcp/MCSE Certification (New York: DDC Publishing, 2000).

Designing a Microsoft Windows 2000 Network Infrastructure with CD-ROM (Redmond, WA: Microsoft Press, 2000).

Managing a Microsoft Windows NT Network: Notes from the Field with CD-ROM (Redmond, WA: Microsoft Press, 1999).

MCSE Training Kit: Microsoft Windows 2000 Network Infrasructure Administration (Exam 70-216) with CD-ROM (Redmond, WA: Microsoft Press, 2001).

PERL AND CGI

Birznieks, Gunther, et al. *CGI Programming with Perl*, 2nd Edition (New York: O'Reilly & Associates, Incorporated, 2000).

Brown, Martin C. *Active PERL Developer's Guide* (New York: The McGraw-Hill Companies, 2000).

Castro, Elizabeth. *PERL and CGI for the World Wide Web* (New York: Addison Wesley Longman, Inc., 1998).

Cozens, Simon. *Beginning PERL* (Chicago: Wrox Press, Inc., 2000).

Hamilton, Jacqueline D. *CGI Programming 101: Programming PERL for the World Wide Web* 2nd Edition (Berkeley, CA: CGI101.COM, 2000).

Williams, Peter. *Applied PERL* (New York: Hungry Minds, Incorporated, 2001).

UNIX

Baklarz, George, and Bill Wong. *The DB2 Universal Database V7.1 Certification Guide for UNIX, Linux, Windows, and OS/2 with CD-ROM*, 4th edition (New York: Prentice-Hall, 2000).

VISUAL BASIC (VB) AND C++

Appleman, Dan, and Jonathan D. Morrison. *C++ for VB Programmers* (Berkeley, CA: Apress Books, 2000).

Bock, Jason, et al. *Beginning VB Application Development* (Chicago: Wrox Press, Inc., 2000).

Gehtland, Justin, et al. *Effective Visual Basic: How to Improve Your VB/Com+ Applications* (New York: Addison Wesley Longman, Inc., 2000).

Getz, Ken, et al. *Access 2000 and VB Language*, 2nd Edition (Alameda, CA: Sybex, Incorporated, 2000).

Hummel, Joe, and Bartosz Milewski. *C++ in Action: Industrial-Strength Programming Techniques with CD* (New York: Addison Wesley Longman, Inc., 2001).

Koenig, Andrew, and Barbara E. Moo. *Accelerated C++: Practical Programming by Example* (New York: Addison Wesley Longman, Inc., 2000).

Nield, Dorothy L. *Microsoft Visual Basic 6.0 Certification Guide: Introduction to Programming* (New York: Thomson Learning, 2000).

Salvage, Jeff. *The C++ Coach: Essentials for Introductory Programming* (New York: Addison Wesley Longman, Inc., 2000).

Wright, Charles. *1001 Visual C++ Programming Tips with CD-ROM* (Schoolcraft, MI: Prima Communications, Inc., 2001).

CAREER AND JOB HUNTING GUIDANCE

Print

Bolles, Richard Nelson. *What Color Is Your Parachute? 2000: A Practical Manual for Job Hunters and Career Changers* (Berkeley, CA: Ten Speed Press, 1999).

Graber, Steven. *The Everything Get-A-Job Book: From Resumé Writing to Interviewing to Finding Tons of Job Openings* (Holbrook, MA: Adams Media Corporation, 2000).

Rich, Jason R. *Your Career: Coach Yourself to Success* (New York: LearningExpress, 2001).

————. *Great Interview: Successful Strategies for Getting Hired* (New York: LearningExpress, 2000).

————. *Great Resume: Get Noticed, Get Hired* (New York: LearningExpress, 2000).

————. *The Unofficial Guide to Earning What You Deserve* (New York: Macmillan, 1999).

————. *Job Hunting for the Utterly Confused* (New York: McGraw-Hill, 1998).

Rothman, Wendy Alfus, and Kate Wendleton. *Targeting the Job You Want: Featuring Special Sections throughout on Using the Internet to Identify and Reach Your Job Targets* (New York: Career Press, Incorporated, 2000).

Smith, Rebecca. *Electronic Resumes & Online Networking: How to Use the Internet to Do a Better Job Search, Including Complete, Up-to-date Resource Guide* (New York: Career Press, 1999).

Online

BrassRing.com	www.brassring.com
computerjobs.com	www.computerjobs.com
dice.com	www.dice.com
HotJobs	www.hotjobs.com
IT*CareerNET™	www.itcareernet.com
Monster Board	www.monster.com
New York New Media Association	www.nynma.org

Techies.com	www.techies.com
TechieGold.com	www.techiegold.com
VirtualJobs.com	www.virtualjobs.com
The Web Career Research Center	www.cio.com/forums/carees
Webmaster-jobs.NET	www.webmaster-jobs.org
webjobsUSA.com	www.webjobsusa.com

INDUSTRY MAGAZINES

Print

AlleyCat News
eCompany now
Electronic Commerce News
E-Vantage
Financial NetNews
The Industry Standard
Macworld
Maximum PC
netWorker
PC Magazine
PC World
Red Herring
SQL Server Magazine
Wired
Yahoo! Internet Life

Online

BigPipe/Cable Today	www.cabletoday.com
Byte.com	www.byte.com
C/Net	www.cnet.com
CIO magazine	www.cio.com/CIO
CIO WebBusiness	webbusiness.cio.com

ClieNT Server News	www.computerwire.com
Computer Reseller News	www.crn.com
Computer Retail Week	www.crw.com
Computer Shopper	www5.zdnet.com/cshopper
Computer User	www.computeruser.com
Computerworld	208.184.36.144
Crossroads: The International ACM Student Magazine	info.acm.org/crossroads
Federal Computer Week	www.fcw.com
HotWired Online Magazine	www.wired.com
InformationWeek	www.informationweek.com
InfoWorld	www.infoworld.com
Internet Week	www.phillips.com/iw
Internet World	www.internetworld.com
IT Support News	www.itsupportnews.com
LAN Magazine	www.lanmag.com
Microsoft Magazine	www.microsoft.com/insider/default.htm
Microsoft Systems Journal	www.microsoft.com/msj/default.asp
PC Week	www.pcweek.com
PC World	www.pcworld.com
Silicon Valley Daily	www.svdaily.com
TechWeb	www.techweb.com
TechWeek	www.techweek.com
The CPA Software News	www.softwarenews.net
Time Digital	www.time.com/time/digital
VAR Business	www.varbusiness.com
Washington Technology Online	www.wtonline.com
Web Week/Internet World	www.webweek.com
WebServer Online	www.cpg.com/ws
Windows Magazine	www.winmag.com
Windows Sources	www.zdnet.com/wsources
Winmag.com	www.winmag.com
Wireless Week	www.wirelessweek.com
ZD Smart Business	www.zdnet.com/pccomp

ADDITIONAL ONLINE RESOURCES

@brint.com (The BizTech Network)	www.brint.com
CMP net	www.cmpnet.com
Duvigneaud.Net	www.duvigneaud.net
Earthweb	www.earthweb.com
Free Academy of Career Training	www.freeacademy.com/ WEBMA.HTM
Webmaster (The Resource for Webmasters)	www.webmastersites.com
HotWired's Webmonkey	www.hotwired.com/webmonkey
HowToWeb	www.howtoweb.com
InfoWorld.com	www.howtoweb.com/corner
Internet Technology Training Center	www.getontheworldwideweb.com
Internet.com	www.internet.com
i-Way Solutions	www.iwaysol.com
Netologist	www.netologist.com
Network Computing	www.networkcomputing.com
New Media Internship Program	www.nynma-internship.org
PlanetIT	www.planetit.com
SitePoint	www.sitepoint.com
tila.com	www.tila.com
The Web Academy	www.webacademy.com
Web Developer's™ Virtual Library	www.wdvl.com
Web Developer.com	www.webdeveloper.com
Webmaster Central	www.todaystechnologies.com/ wmc/index.shtml
Webmaster Yellow Pages	www.webmasteryellowpages.com
WebReference.com	www.webreference.com
The Webmaster's Net	www.thewebmasters.net
Webmasters Seminar Inc.	www.webmasterseminars.com
World Wide Web Consortium	www.w3.org

Appendix C

Educational Accrediting Agencies

NATIONAL EDUCATIONAL ACCREDITING AGENCIES

Accrediting Council for Independent Colleges
and Schools (ACICS)
750 First Street NE, Suite 980
Washington, DC 20002-4242
202-336-6780
Fax: 202-842-2593

Accrediting Commission of Career Schools
and Colleges of Technology
750 First Street NE, Suite 905
Washington, DC 20002-4242
202-336-6850
Fax: 202-842-2585

Accrediting Commission of Distance
Education and Training Council
1601 18th Street NW
Washington, DC 20009-2529
202-234-5100
Fax: 202-332-1386

National Association of Trade and Technical
Schools (NATTS)
2251 Wisconsin Avenue NW
Washington, DC 20009
202-333-1021

National Home Study Council (NHSC)
1601 Eighteenth Street NW
Washington, DC 20009
202-234-5100

Computing Sciences Accreditation Board
(CSAB)
Two Landmark Square, Suite 209,
Stamford, CT 06901
203-975-1117
Fax: 203-975-1222

REGIONAL ACCREDITATION AGENCIES

Middle States Association of Colleges and
Schools (MSACS)
3624 Market Street
Philadelphia, PA 19104-2680
215-662-5606
Fax: 215-662-5501

New England Association of Schools and
Colleges (NEASC)
209 Burlington Road
Bedford, MA 01730-1433
781-271-0022
Fax: 781-271-0950

North Central Association of Colleges
and Schools (NCACS)
159 North Dearborn Street
Chicago, IL 60601
312-263-0456
Fax: 312-263-7462

Northwest Association of Schools and Colleges (NASC)
Boise State University
1910 University Drive
Boise, ID 83725
208-334-3226
Fax: 208-334-3228

Southern Association of Colleges and Schools
(SACS)
1866 Southern Lane
Decatur, GA 30033-4097
404-679-4500
Fax: 404-679-4558

Western Association of Schools and Colleges
(WASC)
533 Airport Boulevard, Suite 200
Burlingame, CA 94010
415-375-7711
Fax: 415-375-7790

ACCREDITING AGENCY RESPONSIBLE FOR EACH STATE

State	Regional Accrediting Agency	State	Regional Accrediting Agency
Alabama	SACS	Nebraska	NCACS
Alaska	NASC	Nevada	NASC
American Samoa	WASC	New Hampshire	NEASC
Arizona	NCACS	New Jersey	MSACS
Arkansas	NCACS	New Mexico	NCACS
California	WASC	New York	MSACS
Colorado	NCACS	North Carolina	SACS
Connecticut	NEASC	North Dakota	NCACS
Delaware	MSACS	Northern Marianas	WASC
District of Columbia	MSACS	Ohio	NCACS
Florida	SACS	Oklahoma	NCACS
Georgia	SACS	Oregon	NASC
Guam	WASC	Pacific Islands	WASC
Hawaii	WASC	Pennsylvania	MSACS
Idaho	NASC	Puerto Rico	MSACS
Illinois	NCACS	Republic of Panama	MSACS
Indiana	NCACS	Rhode Island	NEASC
Iowa	NCACS	South Dakota	NCACS
Kansas	NCACS	Tennessee	SACS
Kentucky	SACS	Texas	SACS
Louisiana	SACS	U.S. Virgin Islands	MSACS
Maine	NEASC	Utah	NASC
Maryland	MSACS	Vermont	NEASC
Massachusetts	NEASC	Virginia	SACS
Michigan	NCACS	Washington	NASC
Minnesota	NCACS	West Virginia	NCACS
Mississippi	SACS	Wisconsin	NCACS
Missouri	NCACS	Wyoming	NCACS
Montana	NASC		

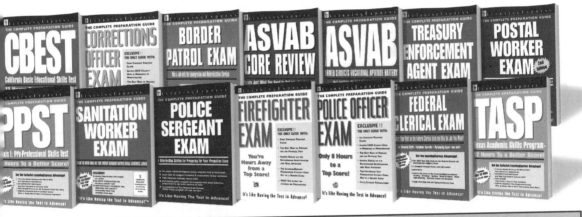